BOOK 2

AQA GCSE ENGLISH LANGUAGE

ASSESSMENT PREPARATION FOR PAPER 1 AND PAPER 2

Jane Branson
Peter Ellison

OXFORD
UNIVERSITY PRESS

OXFORD
UNIVERSITY PRESS

Great Clarendon Street, Oxford, OX2 6DP, United Kingdom

Oxford University Press is a department of the University of Oxford. It furthers the University's objective of excellence in research, scholarship, and education by publishing worldwide. Oxford is a registered trade mark of Oxford University Press in the UK and in certain other countries

© Oxford University Press 2015

First published in 2015.

British Library Cataloguing in Publication Data

Data available

ISBN 978-019-834075-1

10 9 8 7 6

Printed in China by Golden Cup Printing Co. Ltd.

Acknowledgements

The authors and publisher are grateful for permission to reprint extracts from the following copyright material:

Leo Benedictus: 'Inside the supermarkets' dark stores', *theguardian.com*, 7 Jan 2014, copyright © Guardian News & Media Ltd 2014, reprinted by permission of GNM Ltd.

Alan Bennett: *The Lady in the Van* (Faber, 2000), copyright © Alan Bennett 1990, reprinted by permission of Faber & Faber Ltd.

Kevin Brooks: *The Bunker Diary* (Penguin, 2013), copyright © Kevin Brooks 2013, reprinted by permission of Penguin Books Ltd.

Bill Bryson: *The Lost Continent: Travels in Small Town America* (Secker & Warburg, 1989), copyright © Bill Bryson 1989, reprinted by permission of the author.

A S Byatt: 'The Thing in the Forest' from *The Little Black Book of Stories* (Chatto & Windus, 2003), copyright © A S Byatt 2003, reprinted by permission of The Random House Group Ltd.

Philippa Gregory: *The Constant Princess* (HarperCollins, 2006), copyright © Philippa Gregory 2006, reprinted by permission of HarperCollins Publishers, UK.

Jenni Herd: 'Annoyed', letter to *The Times*, 1 March 2014, reprinted by permission of the author.

Susan Hill: *I'm The King of the Castle* (Hamish Hamilton, 1970), copyright © Susan Hill 1970, 1989, reprinted by permission of Sheil Land Associates Ltd.

Stuart Jeffries: 'Is there too much technology in our modern lives?', *The Guardian*, 10 April 2014, copyright © Guardian News & Media Ltd 2014, reprinted by permission of GNM Ltd.

Hari Kunzru: *Transmission* (Hamish Hamilton, 2004), copyright © Hari Kunzru 2004, reprinted by permission of Penguin Books Ltd.

Mary Lawson: *The Other Side of the Bridge* (Chatto & Windus, 2006), copyright © Mary Lawson 2006, reprinted by permission of The Random House Group Ltd, and Lutyens & Rubinstein on behalf of the author.

Laurie Lee: *Cider with Rosie* (Penguin, 1998), copyright © Laurie Lee 1959, reprinted by permission of Curtis Brown Group Ltd, London on behalf of the Estate of Laurie Lee.

Chai Ling: *A Heart for Freedom* (Tyndale House, 2011), reprinted by permission of Tyndale House Publishers.

Tim Lott: 'Why we shouldn't wrap our children in cotton wool', *theguardian. com*, 25 April 2014, copyright © Guardian News & Media Ltd 2014, reprinted by permission of GNM Ltd.

Ian McEwan: *A Child in Time* (Cape, 1987), copyright © Ian McEwan 1987, reprinted by permission of The Random House Group Ltd, and the Author c/o Rogers Coleridge & White Ltd, 20 Powis Mews, London W11 1JN

Julie Myerson: Weekend, '31 ways to enjoy January: Keep a Diary', *The Guardian*, 1 Jan 2005, copyright © Guardian News & Media Ltd 2005, reprinted by permission of GNM Ltd.

Julie Oakley: 'Cheryl Cole take note - My whirlwind marriage has lasted', *theguardian.com*, 15 July 2014, copyright © Guardian News & Media Ltd 2014, reprinted by permission of GNM Ltd.

Vicky Pryce: *Prisonomics: behind bars in Britain's failing prisons* (Biteback, 2013), copyright © Vicky Price 2013, reprinted by permission of Biteback Publishing.

Nigel Slater: *Toast: The story of a boy's hunger* (Fourth Estate, 2003), copyright © Nigel Slater 2003, reprinted by permission of HarperCollins Publishers, UK.

Rupert Thomson: *The Insult* (Bloomsbury, 1996), copyright © Rupert Thomson 1996, reprinted by permission of Bloomsbury Publishing Plc.

Image acknowledgements

The authors and publisher would like to thank the following for permission to use their photographs:

Cover: © Dave Fleetham/Design Pics/Corbis; **p1, 3, 5, 6:** © Dave Fleetham/ Design Pics/Corbis; **p12:** file404/Shutterstock; **p14:** Katrina Wittkamp/ Getty Images; **p15:** © Michele Constantini/PhotoAlto/Corbis; **p16:** Madlen/ Shutterstock; **p17:** Bohbeh/Shutterstock; **p19:** (background) greatstockimages/ Shutterstock, (foreground) Eric Isselee/Shutterstock; **p20:** (t) Steven Bostock/ Shutterstock, (b) Saikom/Shutterstock; **p22:** Sergey Nivens/Shutterstock; **p24:** Anna-Mari West/Shutterstock; **p25:** Lucky Business/Shutterstock; **p26-27:** © Sakis Papadopoulos/Robert Harding World Imagery/Corbis; **p29:** Ana Gram/ Shutterstock; **p28-29:** Serg64/Shutterstock; **p30:** kpatyhka/Shutterstock; **p32:** KsushaArt/Shutterstock; **p35:** © Ron Dahlquist/Design Pics/Corbis; **p36-37:** lorenzobovi/Shutterstock; **p38:** (t) dencg/Shutterstock, (bl) © Mode/Richard Gleed/Alamy; **p38-39:** © AF archive/Alamy; **p39:** © Pictorial Press Ltd/Alamy; **p41:** Mary Evans Picture Library; **p42:** lynea/Shutterstock; **p43:** © Pictorial Press Ltd/Alamy; **p44-45:** 06photo/Shutterstock; **p48-49:** © mediacolor's/ Alamy; **p53:** © Stuart Forster India/Alamy; **p54-55:** RoyStudio.eu/Shutterstock; **p59:** MakiEni's photo/Getty Images; **p61:** Dragon Images/Shutterstock; **p64:** Martina Vaculikova/Shutterstock; **p66:** Kunal Mehta/Shutterstock; **p70:** Feral (2012) provided with kind permission of Daniel Sousa (www.danielsousa. com); **p71:** Ramanchyk Ruslan/Shutterstock; **p72:** Feral (2012) provided with kind permission of Daniel Sousa (www.danielsousa.com); **p74:** Feral (2012) provided with kind permission of Daniel Sousa (www.danielsousa.com); **p76:** BESTWEB/Shutterstock; **p77:** tab62/Shutterstock; **p78:** MarclSchauer/ Shutterstock; **p79:** © Shotshop GmbH/Alamy; **p80:** S_E/Shutterstock; **p83:** © Agencja Fotograficzna Caro/Alamy; **p84:** © Antiques & Collectables/Alamy; **p86:** John Haynes/Lebrecht Music & Arts; **p88:** Antti Metsaranta/Shutterstock and FMStox/Shutterstock; **p89:** JadydangelPhotography/Getty Images; **p90:** © Fanika Zupan/Alamy; **p92-93:** Natalia Davidovich/Shutterstock; **p94:** Kunal Mehta/Shutterstock; **p97:** melis/Shutterstock; **p100:** (background) © Rob Bartee/Alamy, (l) somchaij/Shutterstock, (m) © Photos 12/Alamy; **p102:** Peter Emoke/Shutterstock; **p103:** Mary Evans Picture Library; **p104:** With kind permission of Jenni Herd; **p105:** Mary Evans Picture Library; **p107:** Axel Bueckert/Shutterstock; **p108:** © PhotoAlto/Alamy; **p110:** © Blend Images/ Alamy; **p113:** © FromOldBooks.org/Alamy; **p114-115:** igor.stevanovic/ Shutterstock; **p115:** © Photofusion Picture Library/Alamy; **p116-117:** Mopic/ Shutterstock; **p119:** © The Print Collector/Alamy; **p120:** © RichardBaker/ Alamy; **p122:** © Eyebyte/Alamy; **p125:** Mary Evans Picture Library; **p126:** Mary Evans Picture Library; **p127:** © David Crossland/Alamy; **p128:** Alan Poulson Photography/Shutterstock; **p131:** © Blend Images/Alamy; **p133:** © SOTK2011/ Alamy; **p134:** © Robert Stainforth/Alamy; **p136:** (l) © Pictorial Press Ltd/Alamy, (r) © Justin Kase z03z/Alamy; **p137:** © NEIL SPENCE/Alamy; **p138:** © Heritage Images/Corbis; **p139:** ultimathule/Shutterstock; **p141:** Maridav/Shutterstock; **p142-143:** © A ROOM WITH VIEWS/Alamy; **p143:** Jaguar PS/Shutterstock; **p145:** © The Art Archive/Alamy; **p148:** sakkmesterke/Shutterstock; **p151:** bikeriderlondon/Shutterstock; **p152:** © moodboard/Alamy; **p153:** © dave jepson/Alamy; **p155:** Rawpixel/Shutterstock; **p157:** PathDoc/Shutterstock; **p157, p159:** (margin) Fenton one/Shutterstock; **p160:** © Alexander Maximov/ Alamy; **p163:** © Michael Prince/Corbis; **p164:** Mary Evans Picture Library; **p166:** Mikado767/Shutterstock; **p167:** Myfeel Creative/Shutterstock; **p169:** © Mike Kemp/Tetra Images/Corbis; **p170-171:** natsa/Shutterstock; **p170:** © James Davies/Alamy; **p173:** © ableimages/Alamy; **p174:** (l) Blinka/Shutterstock, (r) Memo Angeles/Shutterstock; **p175:** DankaLilly/Shutterstock; **p178:** Zave Smith/ Getty Images; **p179:** puhhha/Shutterstock; **p180:** Nebojsa Bobic/Shutterstock; **p185:** © Bjanka Kadic/Alamy

With thanks to Kamae Design for artwork and layout.

CONTENTS

AQA GCSE English Language specification overview

The exam papers

The grade you receive at the end of your AQA GCSE English Language course is entirely based on your performance in two exam papers. The following provides a summary of these two exam papers:

Exam paper	Reading and Writing questions and marks	Assessment Objectives	Timing	Marks (and % of GCSE)
Paper 1: Explorations in Creative Reading and Writing	**Section A: Reading** Exam text: • One unseen literature fiction text Exam questions and marks: • One short form question (1 x 4 marks) • Two longer form questions (2 x 8 marks) • One extended question (1 x 20 marks)	Reading: • AO1 • AO2 • AO4	1 hour 45 minutes	Reading: 40 marks (25% of GCSE) Writing: 40 marks (25% of GCSE) Paper 1 total: 80 marks (50% of GCSE)
	Section B: Writing Descriptive or narrative writing Exam question and marks: • One extended writing question (24 marks for content, 16 marks for technical accuracy)	Writing: • AO5 • AO6		
Paper 2: Writers' Viewpoints and Perspectives	**Section A: Reading** Exam text: • One unseen non-fiction text and one unseen literary non-fiction text Exam questions and marks: • One short form question (1 x 4 marks) • Two longer form questions (1 x 8 marks and 1 x 12 marks) • One extended question (1 x 16 marks)	Reading: • AO1 • AO2 • AO3	1 hour 45 minutes	Reading: 40 marks (25% of GCSE) Writing: 40 marks (25% of GCSE) Paper 2 total: 80 marks (50% of GCSE)
	Section B: Writing Writing to present a viewpoint Exam question and marks: • One extended writing question (24 marks for content, 16 marks for technical accuracy)	Writing: • AO5 • AO6		

What sorts of texts and stimulus tasks will the exam papers include?

Paper 1

Section A: Reading will include the following types of text:

- A prose literature text from either the 20th or 21st century
- It will be an extract from a novel or short story.
- It will focus on openings, endings, narrative perspectives and points of view, narrative or descriptive passages, character, atmospheric descriptions and other appropriate narrative and descriptive approaches.

Section B: Writing will include the following stimulus:

- There will be a choice of scenario, either a written prompt or a visual image related to the topic of the reading text in Section A. The scenario sets out a context for writing with a designated audience, purpose and form that will differ to those specified on Paper 2.
- You will produce your own writing, inspired by the topic that you responded to in Section A.

Paper 2

Section A: Reading will include the following types of text:

- Two linked sources (one non-fiction and one literary non-fiction) from different time periods (one 19th century and one from either the 20th or 21st century, depending on the time period of the text in Paper 1) and different genres in order to consider how each presents a perspective or viewpoint to influence the reader.

Section B: Writing will include the following stimulus:

- You will produce a written text to a specified audience, purpose and form in which you give your own perspective on the theme that has been introduced in Section A.

Spoken Language

As well as preparing for the two GCSE English Language exams, your course also includes Spoken Language assessment. This is **not** an exam. Instead your teacher sets and marks the assessments.

There are three separate Assessment Objectives covering Spoken Language – AO7, AO8 and AO9. At the end of your course you will receive a separate endorsement for Spoken Language, which means it will not count as part of your GCSE English Language qualification.

How will you be assessed?

The Assessment Objectives (AOs)

Assessment Objectives are the skills that underpin all qualifications. Your GCSE English Language exam papers are testing six Assessment Objectives – AOs 1-6 – whilst your Spoken Language tests AOs 7-9. The Assessment Objectives for GCSE English Language are as follows:

AO1	• identify and interpret explicit and implicit information and ideas • select and synthesise evidence from different texts
AO2	Explain, comment on and analyse how writers use language and structure to achieve effects and influence readers, using relevant subject terminology to support their views
AO3	Compare writers' ideas and perspectives, as well as how these are conveyed, across two or more texts
AO4	Evaluate texts critically and support this with appropriate textual references
AO5	Communicate clearly, effectively and imaginatively, selecting and adapting tone, style and register for different forms, purposes and audiences. Organise information and ideas, using structural and grammatical features to support coherence and cohesion of texts
AO6	Candidates must use a range of vocabulary and sentence structures for clarity, purpose and effect, with accurate spelling and punctuation.
AO7	Demonstrate presentation skills in a formal setting
AO8	Listen and respond appropriately to spoken language, including to questions and feedback on presentations
AO9	Use spoken Standard English effectively in speeches and presentations.

How will you be assessed in your reading skills?

Your reading skills will be assessed in the Reading sections of Paper 1 and Paper 2. The following chart shows which Reading Assessment Objectives (AOs) are tested in Paper 1 and Paper 2.

Assessment Objectives (AOs)	Paper 1	Paper 2
AO1	✓	✓
AO2	✓	✓
AO3	-	✓
AO4	✓	-

By working through the Reading chapters of this book, you will practise these skills and learn exactly how and where to demonstrate them in the exams in order to achieve your best possible marks.

How will you be assessed in your writing skills?

Your writing skills will be assessed in the Writing sections of Paper 1 and Paper 2. The following chart shows that both Writing AOs are tested in Paper 1 and Paper 2.

Assessment Objectives (AOs)	Paper 1	Paper 2
AO5	✓	✓
AO6	✓	✓

By working through the Writing chapters of this book, you will practise these skills and learn exactly how and where to demonstrate them in the exams in order to achieve your best possible marks.

How are your exam papers marked?

The examiners use mark schemes to mark your exam papers. Each Assessment Objective has its own mark scheme, giving guidance as to the different levels that students might attain in their exam responses. You will see examples of mark scheme levels, together with sample exam answers, throughout this book.

Becoming familiar with these mark schemes will help you assess your own work and that of your peers as well as give you an understanding of what the examiners are looking for. Teachers will also find these mark schemes useful when assessing students' work during the course and in preparation for the examinations.

Each level in the mark schemes also includes 'Skills descriptors' which are specific to each Assessment Objective. Examples of these can be found in this book, in the Teacher Companion and on the AQA website.

Further GCSE English Language and GCSE English Literature resources

AQA GCSE English Language Student Book 1: Developing the Skills for Learning and Assessment

Approved by AQA, Student Book 1 develops vital reading and writing skills in engaging thematic contexts whilst also focusing on the Assessment Objectives linked to the requirements of the exams. This book is ideal for the start of the GCSE course and features:

- in-depth reading and writing skills-development in thematic contexts
- differentiated support and stretch with an embedded focus on technical accuracy
- Assessment Objective focus linked to the requirements of the exams
- opportunities for peer and self-assessment
- regular formative and summative assessments, including sample exam papers.

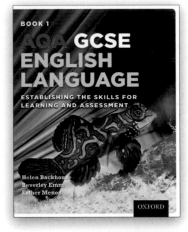

AQA GCSE English Language Student Book 1: Establishing the Skills for Learning and Assessment

This Student Book focuses on establishing students' reading and writing skills and is ideal for the start of the GCSE course. Structured around engaging themes in the context of the Assessment Objectives, with regular formative and summative assessments, and an embedded focus on SPAG, this book also includes:

- the same core structure as Student Book 1: Developing the Skills for Learning and Assessment
- clear and accessible teaching explanations and source texts
- additional support and steps in the activities
- models of writing with a further focus on basic skills and technical accuracy.

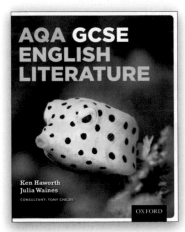

AQA GCSE English Literature Student Book

This Student Book provides in-depth skills development for the English Literature specification, including:

- comprehensive coverage and practice of the poetry anthology and unseen poetry requirements
- advice and activities to support Shakespeare, the 19th-century novel and modern prose and drama
- sample student responses at different levels and sample exam-style tasks to help prepare you for the exam paper questions
- Stretch and Support features to ensure all students make progress
- clear, student-friendly explanations of the Assessment Objectives and the skills required to meet them

AQA GCSE English Language and English Literature Teacher Companion

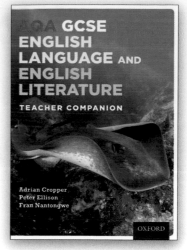

The Teacher Companion provides support for teachers to help them plan and deliver their GCSE programme, including:

- specification insight and planning guidance to aid planning and delivery of the specifications
- teaching tips and guidance for effective lesson delivery to all students of the material in Student Book 1, with additional support for differentiation and personalization
- exam preparation guidance and planning, with links to English Language Student Book 2 and English Literature Student Book
- links to, and guidance on, the additional resources on Kerboodle.

AQA GCSE English Language and English Literature Kerboodle: Resources and Assessment

What is Kerboodle?

Kerboodle is a brand new online subscription-based platform provided by Oxford University Press.

Kerboodle: Resources and Assessment

This AQA GCSE English Language and English Literature Kerboodle: Resources and Assessment provides support and resources to enable English departments and individual teachers to plan their GCSE courses and deliver effective, personalized lessons. Resources include:

- Teaching and learning materials, linked to the corresponding Student Books and Teacher Companion, including:
  - Differentiation, personalization and peer/self-assessment worksheets and teaching resources
  - A bank of assignable spelling, punctuation and grammar interactive activities to improve technical accuracy
- Assessment resources, including:
  - Marked sample answers and mark schemes
  - Editable versions of the end-of-chapter Student Book assessments and sample exam papers

- Professional development materials, including:
  - Seven specially-commissioned film-based CPD units devised by Geoff Barton, with classroom lesson footage, additional interviews and supporting written resources
  - A grammar guide for GCSE teaching
- Planning resources, including:
  - Editable sample schemes of work and medium-term plans, with guidance on what to consider when planning your GCSE course
  - CPD units supporting discussion around departmental GCSE planning
- Digital books, including:
  - Student Books 1 and 2, and the English Literature Student Book in digital format
  - A bank of tools enabling personalization

Reading a substantial text in an exam

Before we consider how best to answer Question 1, we need to think about the most effective way to read the source text.

Type of extract

You will be expected to read a substantial passage of fiction taken from a novel or a short story. This might be:

- a story opening
- a story ending
- a description of a scene or an event
- a description of one or more characters.

Extracts will have been chosen to show how established writers use narrative and descriptive techniques to capture the interest of readers.

What to expect in the exam

There will always be a sentence or two that introduces the source text, giving you some information about what you are going to read. Don't skip this, because it will be helpful in preparing you for what follows.

Look at the following example of this introductory text:

In this episode from a novel by Ian McEwan, Stephen, a young father, has taken his three-year-old daughter Kate to the supermarket and they have reached the checkout.

> ### Activity 1
>
> Copy out the sentence above. Note down any thoughts about what you might expect the extract to contain.

It is important to learn as much as you can from your first reading of the text. It will be fiction but you need to think about its genre, content, setting and tone as you read.

Now read the following extract from the novel *A Child in Time* by Ian McEwan.

> Kate was holding on to the wide bar at the
> other end of the trolley, pretending to push.
> There was no one behind her. Now the person
> immediately ahead of Stephen, a man with a
> 5 curved back, was about to pay for several tins
> of dog food. Stephen lifted the first items on

to the belt. When he straightened he might have been conscious of a figure in a dark coat behind Kate. But it was hardly an awareness at all, it was the weakest suspicion brought to life by a desperate memory. The coat could have been a dress or a
10 shopping bag or his own invention. He was intent on ordinary tasks, keen to finish them. He was barely a conscious being at all.

The man with the dog food was leaving. The checkout girl was already at work, the fingers of one hand flickering over the keypad while the other drew Stephen's items towards her. As he took the salmon from the trolley he glanced down at Kate and
15 winked. She copied him, but clumsily, wrinkling her nose and closing both eyes. He set the fish down and asked the girl for a carrier bag. She reached under a shelf and pulled one out. He took it and turned. Kate was gone. There was no one in the queue behind him. Unhurriedly he pushed the trolley clear, thinking she had ducked down behind the end of the counter. Then he took a few paces and glanced down
20 the only aisle she would have had time to reach. He stepped back and looked to his left and right. On one side there were lines of shoppers, on the other a clear space, then the chrome turnstile, then the automatic doors on to the pavement. There may have been a figure in a coat hurrying away from him, but at that time Stephen was looking for a three-year-old child, and his immediate worry was the traffic.

25 This was a theoretical, precautionary anxiety. As he shouldered past shoppers and emerged on to the broad pavement he knew he would not see her there. Kate was not adventurous in this way. She was not a strayer. She was too sociable, she preferred the company of the one she was with. She was also terrified of the road. He turned back and relaxed. She had to be in the shop, and she could come to no
30 real harm there. He expected to see her emerging from behind the lines of shoppers at the checkouts. It was easy enough to overlook a child in the first flash of concern, to look too hard, too quickly. Still, a sickness and a tightening at the base of the throat, an unpleasant lightness in the feet, were with him as he went back. When he walked past all the tills, ignoring the girl at his who was irritably trying to attract his
35 attention, a chill rose to the top of his stomach. At a controlled run – he was not yet past caring how foolish he looked – he went down all the aisles, past mountains of oranges, toilet rolls, soup. It was not until he was back at his starting point that he abandoned all propriety, filled his constricted lungs and
40 shouted Kate's name.

Now he was taking long strides, bawling her name as he pounded the length of an aisle and headed once more for the door. Faces were turning towards him. There was no mistaking him for one of the drunks who blundered in to buy cider. His fear
45 was too evident, too forceful, it filled the impersonal, fluorescent space with unignorable human warmth. Within moments all shopping around him had ceased. Baskets and trolleys were set aside, people were converging and saying Kate's name and somehow, in no time at all, it was generally known that she was
50 three, that she was last seen at the checkout, that she wore green dungarees and carried a toy donkey.

The following activities are designed to help you get used to drawing out the main points of a text that you read. You will not need to do these activities during the exam itself.

Activity 2

Copy and complete the table below, to explore the extract from *A Child in Time* on pages 14–15.

Genre, e.g. historical or contemporary?	
Content, e.g. events and characters	
Setting	
Tone	

Activity 3

a Imagine that the extract on pages 14–15 has appeared on an exam paper. With a partner, develop your thinking about the extract:

• Discuss what you think the main focus of the questions might be.

• Come up with at least one question that you think might be on the exam paper including the words 'how' and 'language'.

b Which of the following words and phrases do you think are likely to be featured in any answer on this extract:

| fear | relief | anger | childhood | queuing |

| rising panic | a disobedient child | bad parenting |

| parental concern | changing atmosphere |

c If you had to split the extract into three sections, where would you divide it?

• Use the line numbers to indicate which line would start each section.

• Give each section an appropriate subheading.

• Explain the reasons for your decisions.

The key to success in reading a substantial passage in an exam is practice.
Repeat the following activity as many times as you can.

Activity 4

a Go into the school or class library and select a novel from the shelf and open it at random on a double-page spread.

b Read the extract as quickly as you can, satisfying yourself that you have understood it as far as you are able.

c Now put it down and describe what you have read to a partner or note your thoughts down on paper.

Question 1

What to expect in the exam

In the exam, Question 1 refers to a section of the text and is worth four marks. It addresses AO1 and is a straightforward task, designed to test that you can read a small section of the text and select key pieces of information from it.

Unlike the other questions on this paper, there are no levels used in the Mark Scheme. You simply receive a single mark for each correct piece of information. Either the information you have identified is correct or it is not.

Like many seemingly straightforward tasks, however, Question 1 can pose some difficulties. Bear in mind the following:

- You might be a little nervous at the beginning of the exam.
- The text is fiction and the information might be embedded within detailed description.
- The question will direct you to a specific part of the text, using line numbers. Make sure that you only select information from the identified lines. Any information, even if correct, from outside those lines will not gain a mark.
- You may find more than four pieces of information. Don't spend too long wondering which ones to write down. For this question any correct pieces of information will gain you marks.
- Some students worry that the answers seem too obvious to be correct. Don't worry. This first question is intended to be straightforward. Don't spend any more time on it than is absolutely necessary.

Identifying explicit information

The information that you will be asked to find for this question is likely to be **explicit** – in other words, clearly stated in the text.

So how do you go about identifying explicit information in a piece of fiction?

We tend to think of fiction as telling a story and of course, that is true; however, in order to build up a picture in the reader's mind, writers need to inform us. They must tell us what sort of place we are in (the setting), who the main characters are and what they are like (characterization) and what is happening (the action).

Read the extract on page 19 and then complete Activity 1.

In Susan Hill's novel *I'm the King of the Castle*, a young boy, Kingshaw, has decided to run away from home. He sets out across the fields towards a wood.

The cornfield was high up. He stood in the very middle of it, now, and the sun came glaring down. He could feel the sweat running over his back, and in the creases of his thighs. His face was burning. He sat down, although the stubble pricked at him, through his jeans, and looked over at the dark line of trees on the edge of Hang
5   Wood. They seemed very close – all the individual branches were clearly outlined. The fields around him were absolutely still.

When he first saw the crow, he took no notice. There had been several crows. This one glided down into the corn on its enormous, ragged black wings. He began to be aware of it when it rose up suddenly, circled overhead, and then dived, to land not very far
10   away from him. Kingshaw could see the feathers on its head, shining black in between the butter-coloured corn-stalks. Then it rose, and circled, and came down again, this time not quite landing, but flapping about his head, beating its wings and making a sound like flat leather pieces being slapped together. It was the largest crow he had ever seen. As it came down for the third time, he looked up and noticed its beak,
15   opening in a screech. The inside of its mouth was scarlet, it had small glinting eyes.

Kingshaw got up and flapped his arms. For a moment, the bird retreated a little way off, and higher up in the sky. He began to walk rather quickly back, through the path in the corn, looking ahead of him. Stupid to be scared of a rotten bird. What could a bird do? But he felt his own extreme isolation, high up in the cornfield.

20   For a moment, he could only hear the soft thudding of his own footsteps, and the silky sound of the corn, brushing against him. Then, there was a rush of air, as the great crow came beating down, and wheeled about his head. The beak opened and the hoarse caaw came out again and again, from inside the scarlet mouth.

Activity 1

a Re-read the second paragraph of the above extract from *I'm the King of the Castle* (lines 7–15).

b List *four* things about the crow's appearance and behaviour that Kingshaw finds frightening.

c Compare your choices with a partner. Did you both choose the same information?

Listed below are some possible answers for the previous activity.

- It was very large.
- It had enormous ragged black wings.
- It rose up suddenly.
- It flapped about his head.
- It beat its wings noisily.
- It kept diving towards him.
- It screeched.
- Its mouth was scarlet inside.
- It had glinting eyes.

Notice that some information is **paraphrased** and some is directly quoted. This is because the question is not concerned with the precise language used to describe the crow, only the information. You will get a mark for a correct piece of information whether you write it down paraphrased or quoted.

Key term 🔑

Paraphrased: reworded, explained in a different way

Try it yourself (on your own)

Tip ✓

In the exam, write just one answer against each letter or number given. Do not be tempted to write more.

Activity 2

Re-read the first paragraph of the source text *A Child in Time* on pages 14–15 and complete the example of a Question 1 task below.

> List *four* things that the narrator notices, or thinks that he notices, before Kate disappears.
>
> **[4 marks]**

Progress check

So far you have learned how to approach the fiction text and Question 1 by focusing on the key skills of:

- reading with understanding
- identifying explicit information.

a Now see how confident you are with these skills by completing the self-assessment below.

Skills	I am confident that I can do this.	I think I can do this but need a bit more practice.	This is one of my weaker areas, so I need more practice.
1. I can identify the genre of a text.			
2. I can identify the main content of a text.			
3. I can identify the setting of a text.			
4. I can identify the tone of a text.			
5. I can select relevant pieces of explicit information.			
6. I can quote from the text or paraphrase the information.			

b Pick out one skill that you would like to target for improvement. Plan how you will improve that skill and monitor your progress. For example:

Plan – practise selecting relevant information from a fiction text.

Monitor – work with a partner at regular intervals to select information from a fiction text and compare answers.

Question 2

Assessment Objective

AO2

● Explain, comment on and analyse how writers use *language* … to achieve effects

What to expect in the exam

Question 2 refers to a section of the text and is worth 8 marks. It addresses AO2 and is much more demanding than Question 1. Where Question 1 asks you to select *what* is in the text, this question asks you to look at *how* the writer uses language to describe an event.

AO2 assesses your ability to:

Explain, comment on and analyse how writers use language and structure to achieve effects and influence readers, using relevant subject terminology to support their views.

This question, however, only focuses on one part of the AO; the use of language.

You will be asked to think about and comment on:

● words and phrases

● language features and techniques

● sentence forms.

The key skills that you need to show when you answer a language question are:

- *Selecting* relevant examples of words and phrases, language features and techniques and *identifying* effective sentence forms
- *Commenting* on them and *analysing* them.

An extract from the Mark Scheme that examiners use to mark Question 2 is printed below. There are four levels. The key words for each level are printed on the left-hand side and the skills that you have to demonstrate in your response are on the right. Notice the words in bold which identify the differences between each level.

Level	Skill descriptors
Level 4 Perceptive, detailed 7–8 marks	Show **detailed** and **perceptive** understanding of *language* • **Analyses** the effect of the writer's choices of *language* • Selects a **judicious** range of quotations • Uses **sophisticated** subject terminology accurately
Level 3 Clear, relevant 5–6 marks	Shows **clear** understanding of *language* • **Clearly explains** the effects of the writer's choice of *language* • Selects a range of **relevant** quotations • Uses subject terminology **accurately**
Level 2 Some, attempts 3–4 marks	Shows **some** understanding of *language* • **Attempts to comment** on the effect of *language* • **Selects some** relevant quotations • Uses some subject terminology, **not always appropriately**
Level 1 Simple, limited 1–2 marks	Shows **simple** awareness of *language* • Offers **simple comment** on the effect of *language* • **Simple references** or textual details • **Simple mention** of subject terminology

Annotations:
- explores and explains in depth and detail
- correctly and precisely
- deep, clever and high level
- well chosen and appropriate
- high level
- related to what is being discussed or dealt with

Now let's look at the next part of the same passage from *I'm the King of the Castle*. Focus on Susan Hill's skill with language, thinking about the following question:

> In lines 16–23, *how* does the writer use language to make us feel Kingshaw's fear?

First, we'll concentrate on selecting relevant examples of language from the first paragraph (lines 16–19). As you are reading, ask yourself the following question:

Which are the most important words and phrases that convey fear?

16 Kingshaw got up and flapped his arms. For a moment, the bird retreated a little way off, and higher up in the sky. He began to walk rather quickly back, through the path in the corn, looking ahead of him. Stupid to be scared of a rotten bird. What could a
19 bird do? But he felt his own extreme isolation, high up in the cornfield.

Activity 2

a Copy out the paragraph above on a large sheet of paper, using double line spacing, and underline any words or phrases that you think contribute to the reader's understanding of Kingshaw's fear.

b In a different colour, identify and annotate any techniques that Hill uses (go back to the table of literary language features in Activity 1 to remind yourself).

c In another colour, highlight any sentence forms that Hill uses to communicate Kingshaw's fear. (Refer back to the table of grammar features, if you need a reminder.)

d Compare your annotations with a partner and talk through the reasons for your selections.

Analysing language features

Activity 3

The following table contains three examples that you may have selected in Activity 2.

a Copy it out and complete the commentary sections in as much detail as you can. One example has been completed for you.

Language	Examples	Commentary
Words and phrases	'rather quickly' 'looking ahead of him'	This tells us that he is still scared and is trying to escape. He's too frightened of the crow to look up and he thinks that it will attack again.
Language features and techniques	He 'flapped' his arms	
Sentence forms	She writes Kingshaw's thoughts as if he is speaking aloud: 'Stupid to be scared of a rotten bird. What could a bird do?'	

b When you have completed both commentaries, compare your table with a partner. How do your commentaries compare?

Now read the following extract from Student A's response to this question.

Student A

Kingshaw 'flapped' his arms, a verb which indicates his panic. At first it seems to work and the bird 'retreated'. When Kingshaw sets off again he 'walks quickly', 'looking ahead of him'. This suggests that he is keen to get away from the crow and is too frightened to look up in case he sees it. Hill now introduces Kingshaw's thoughts to show how he is trying to calm himself. Hill writes these as if he is speaking aloud, 'Stupid to be scared of a rotten bird' and the rhetorical question 'What could a bird do?' which shows us that he is trying to persuade himself that it isn't dangerous.

This sample would be placed in a low Level 3 because it:

Shows **clear** understanding of language
- **Clearly** explains the effects of the writer's choices of language
- Selects a range of **relevant** quotations
- Uses subject terminology **accurately**

So, let's analyse how Student A has achieved a Level 3.

Activity 4

a Copy out Student A's answer and highlight in yellow the words, phrases, language features and sentence forms that the student has selected.

b In a second colour, highlight the analysis and commentary.

c Use a third colour to highlight any subject terminology.

d Compare your highlighting with a partner.

Student A's answer is good but it could be improved. Now read a sample taken from Student B's response.

Student B

The first two sentences of the paragraph contain some effective verbs which convey Kingshaw's fear. We are told that he 'flapped' his arms in panic, which is ironic because it mimics the action of a bird, rather than what we think of as a normal action of a human. We're then told that the crow 'retreated' which makes us think of the crow as an enemy army that has been beaten and so is moving back in order to re-group. The use of 'for a moment' anticipates the next attack. We know that the crow hasn't been beaten.

Kingshaw walks 'rather quickly back', 'looking ahead of him', which suggests that he is still scared and worried that if he looks up he will see the crow again. It's as if he would really like to run but would be ashamed to seem so scared of a crow. This feeling is strengthened when Hill reveals Kingshaw's thoughts, 'Stupid to be scared of a rotten bird. What could a bird do?'; he is telling himself off for being scared, describing the bird as 'rotten' to make it seem unimportant and trying to convince himself that he isn't really scared.

In the final line of the paragraph, Hill reminds us of his 'isolation', making him seem like a tiny animal that is alone, vulnerable and exposed to attack.

This answer would be placed in a low Level 4 because it:

Shows **detailed** and **perceptive** understanding of language
- **Analyses** the effects of the writer's choices of language
- Selects a **judicious** range of quotations
- Uses **sophisticated** subject terminology accurately

Activity 5

a In a pair or small group, read through Student A and Student B's responses again.

b Compare the two answers. What has Student B done that Student A hasn't? Look for *detail*, *perception* (noticing small things) and *analysis* (deep thought).

Now we'll look at the second paragraph. Re-read lines 16–23 from the extract.

> 16 Kingshaw got up and flapped his arms. For a moment, the bird retreated a little way off, and higher up in the sky. He began to walk rather quickly back, through the path in the corn, looking ahead of him. Stupid to be scared of a rotten bird. What could a bird do? But he felt his own extreme isolation, high up in the cornfield.
>
> 20 For a moment, he could only hear the soft thudding of his own footsteps, and the silky sound of the corn, brushing against him. Then, there was a rush of air, as the great crow came beating down, and wheeled about his head. The beak opened and the hoarse caaw came out again and again, from inside the scarlet mouth.

Activity 6

a Continue Student B's response, addressing the second paragraph (lines 20–23). Can you keep the answer in Level 4?

b When you have finished, compare your answer with a partner. Read each other's work. Can you persuade your partner that your answer should remain in Level 4?

To improve the quality of your answers to AO2 questions such as this, you should practise analysing small amounts of text (no more than a single paragraph). Think of it as if you are squeezing or wringing the last drop of meaning from the passage.

Activity 7

To practise squeezing out meaning, try this:

a Pick a novel at random from a library shelf.

b Flick through the pages until you find a passage that is descriptive narrative with no (or little) dialogue.

c Select a paragraph and squeeze out as much meaning from it as you can. You'll be amazed at how much a good writer can pack into a short space.

Try it yourself (with support)

Now you are going to practise using all the skills you have learned so far in a complete response to Question 2. You'll be given some support to help you do this. First of all, look back over pages 22–29 to remind yourself of how to approach the question, then read the following extract from *A Child in Time* that you read on pages 14–15.

This was a theoretical, precautionary anxiety. As he shouldered past shoppers and emerged on to the broad pavement he knew he would not see her there. Kate was not adventurous in this way. She was not
5 a strayer. She was too sociable, she preferred the company of the one she was with. She was also terrified of the road. He turned back and relaxed. She had to be in the shop, and she could come to no real harm there. He expected to see her emerging from behind the lines
10 of shoppers at the checkouts. It was easy enough to overlook a child in the first flash of concern, to look too hard, too quickly. Still, a sickness and a tightening at the base of the throat, an unpleasant lightness in the feet, were with him as he went back. When he walked
15 past all the tills, ignoring the girl at his who was irritably trying to attract his attention, a chill rose to the top of his stomach. At a controlled run – he was not yet past caring how foolish he looked – he went down all the aisles, past mountains of oranges, toilet rolls, soup. It
20 was not until he was back at his starting point that he abandoned all propriety, filled his constricted lungs and shouted Kate's name.

Activity 8

Complete the following example of a Question 2 task using the extract opposite.

> How does the writer use language here to convey the father's increasing anxiety?
>
> Remember to analyse the writer's choice of:
>
> - words and phrases
> - language features and techniques
> - sentence forms.

When completing your response, remember to:

- select a range of quotations to support your analysis
- use subject terminology correctly to identify the writer's techniques.

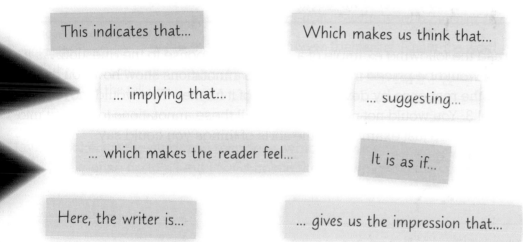

This indicates that...

Which makes us think that...

... implying that...

... suggesting...

... which makes the reader feel...

It is as if...

Here, the writer is...

... gives us the impression that...

Peer assessment

Activity 9

a Swap your response with a partner. Does your partner's response:

- analyse the writer's use of language (words, phrases, language features and techniques and sentence forms)?
- select the most appropriate quotations to support the analysis?
- use subject terminology correctly to identify techniques and features?

b Make some notes on what your partner has done successfully and what could be improved.

c Now spend a few minutes giving your partner some feedback.

Progress check

So far, you have learned how to approach Question 2 by:

- identifying language features
- selecting effective examples to support your answer
- commenting on them and analysing them using subject terminology.

a Now see how confident you are with these skills by completing the self-assessment below.

Skills	I am confident that I can do this.	I think I can do this but need a bit more practice.	This is one of my weaker areas, so I need more practice.
1. I can identify language features in a text.			
2. I can select effective examples to comment on and analyse.			
3. I can comment on and analyse language features using subject terminology.			

b Pick out one skill that you would like to target for improvement. Plan how you will improve that skill and monitor your progress. For example:

Plan – practise using correct subject terminology to identify language features in a text.

Monitor – work with a partner at regular intervals to test each other on subject terminology and identifying relevant examples in a text.

Tip ✓

Re-read the full Mark Scheme (on page 23) before you complete this task. It will help you to remember what is being assessed.

Try it yourself (on your own)

Read the extract opposite from *The Insult* by Rupert Thomson and write a response to the Question 2 task below it, applying all the skills you have learned.

And that was when it happened.

One evening I was crossing the lawn, feeling as if I knew each mound, each root, each blade of grass by heart, when I realised that what lay in front of me – what I could 'see', as it were – was not the usual grey, featureless and empty. *It was green,*
5   *and there were shapes in it.* You must be imagining it, I told myself. This is one of the illusions Visser warned you about. You think you're seeing, but you're not.

I stood quite still and looked around me.

The shapes in the green were trees. And I could see the lawn, too, reaching away from me, then sloping down. There was a smoothness at the end of it. A lake. I could
10 see a stand of poplars, tapering like rockets as they lifted into the sky.

The sky!

For a moment I didn't dare to move in case it all cut out and I went blind again. Then I knew what I would do. I chose one tree and slowly began to walk towards it. The tree grew larger. At last I was close enough to touch it. I reached out. There was bark
15 beneath my fingers, ridged and damp. I looked up. Leaves shifting in the evening wind.

This was no illusion. I was seeing the tree, the gardens – everything. *I was seeing.* I stood there with the tips of my fingers touching bark. Leaves turned and turned above my head – the rush of blood through arteries.

20 I couldn't move.

Activity (12)

Look in detail at lines 1–20 of the source.

In this extract from Rupert Thomson's novel *The Insult*, the narrator has been shot and blinded. His doctor, Dr Visser, has told him that he will never see again.

How does the writer use language here to describe the narrator's experience of being able to see again?

You could include the writer's choice of:

• words and phrases
• language features and techniques
• sentence forms.

[8 marks]

What is the structure of an extract?

It's likely that throughout your time at school you will have been asked to consider the use of language in a text many times; the structure, however, may not be such familiar territory. So, what do we mean by the term 'structure' and how we can identify its features?

When a writer is planning a piece of fiction, he or she must think about guiding the reader through it in a way that makes it clear and effective. Ideas must be introduced in an order which creates vivid images in the reader's mind and helps them to 'see' what the writer intends. This is similar to the way that a film director structures a film, by selecting camera shots.

Activity 1

a Watch the beginning of a film you know well and use the following table to help you to note down how the first scene is structured.

Setting	How do we know where the film is set? Do we see outside or inside a building?
Character	How do we know who the main character is? Do we see him/her immediately or is he or she introduced later?
Atmosphere	Is the scene light or dark? What sort of colours are used?
Events	What happens in the first few minutes? How do the events involve the viewer?

b Now think about the order in which each aspect is brought in. Does the film start with the setting or the character? How do we learn important information in the first scene?

The text you are given in this exam *may* come from the opening of a book, so think about what a writer needs to do in the first few pages to capture the reader's interest.

Every novel is like a small world created by its author. The reader's introduction to this world is crucial to the success of any novel. If we don't understand or like this world, we won't read on. In fact, the opening of a novel is even more important than the first scene of a film because we often choose to buy a book simply on the basis of whether we like the opening. If the opening fails, the book will fail, so authors and editors spend a great deal of time on getting the structure of the opening right.

Activity 2

a Choose a novel at random from a library shelf. With a partner, read the first two or three pages.

b Discuss how the writer has attempted to capture your interest. Consider similar questions to the ones you addressed when you talked about the film:

Setting	How do we know when and where the book is set? Are we outside or inside a building?
Narrator	Is it a first- or a third-person narrator?
Character	How is the main character introduced? Do we meet him/her immediately or is he or she introduced later?
Atmosphere	Is the atmosphere light or dark? Does it change during the passage?
Events	What happens in the first few pages? How do the events engage the reader?

c Now introduce your book to another group, explaining how the writer has captured the reader's interest and created the 'world' of the novel. Talk about the choices the writer has made about what to show you and when. Explain when the author makes things move, shift and change, like a camera operator taking you, the reader, with him or her.

d We can look at structure in any part of a novel or story, not just at the beginning. Open your selected book at a random double-page spread and identify how the passage is structured. What do we see, hear and feel first? How does it change over the course of the two pages?

39

Activity 8

a Now swap your response with a partner. Does your partner's response:

- analyse the writer's use of structural features, such as beginnings/introductions/developments/perspective and place shifts/changes of topic with new paragraphs/variety of paragraph lengths/links between paragraphs?

- select the most appropriate quotations to support the analysis?

- use subject terminology correctly to identify techniques and features?

b Make some notes on what your partner has done successfully and what could be improved.

c Now spend a few minutes giving your partner some feedback.

Improving your answer

Now read the following example of a complete response to the question in Activity 7, on page 43. As it stands, it would be placed in Level 3, but the annotations show how you could improve the response by developing parts of it further. This would move it up into Level 4. You would not need to include all these annotations to move it into Level 4; they are just examples of the sorts of things you could say.

You could add ' – that the father is straining to remember details for a reason', to show that the reader is beginning to predict that something dreadful might happen.

This would be a good opportunity to comment on the change of focus: we go from a wide viewpoint of what's happening in the supermarket, to a close-up focus getting inside the father's mind.

Add in: 'It is as if we are in his body as he paces and strides through the supermarket, his movement reflecting his mounting anxiety.' This shows the shift of focus to the father's physical response to his fear.

The passage begins by focusing on the normality of the visit to the supermarket. Even at this stage, however, the father is trying to remember details of the other shoppers in a way that you wouldn't if this was a boring shopping trip. This alerts us to the possibility that something awful will happen. When the father talks about this being 'a desperate memory', this adds to the sense of disquiet. The details of the figure and the dark coat draw our attention away from the normal, everyday description and make us more alert.

In the second paragraph the father is focused on what is happening in front of him at the checkout. The words 'Kate was gone.' form a single short sentence and so come as a real shock to the reader.

At the word 'traffic', the focus shifts again. It's like a danger signal has flashed on and in the next paragraph the pace increases as he rushes to the street, taking the reader with him. McEwan increases the pace by letting us hear the father's speeding thoughts as he searches. Now the writing takes on a frantic, blurred quality — like a dreadful dream. We continue to hear the father's thoughts as they switch between fear and reassurance. We see the supermarket through the narrator's eyes as he seems separated from the world. At this point the writer introduces the physical symptoms of panic. He is still in control though, until he loses any sense of embarrassment and shouts his daughter's name, which changes the focus again.

Now, 'Faces were turning towards him' and we feel their empathy. As the other shoppers become aware of his situation, the focus draws back. We see the supermarket from a wider angle, with the father at its centre, striding around bawling his daughter's name. Finally, we move away from the father's point of view and join the other shoppers.

A quotation here would help to emphasize the point: 'he might have been conscious of a figure in a dark coat…'.

This comment is more about language than structure; remember that it is comments on *structure* that will give you marks for this question.

Add in: 'This is like a close-up shot of the empty trolley. We start to see the supermarket through the father's eyes, 'on one side…, on the other…' as if we are scanning the supermarket with him.'

Add in: 'and it is as if the scene freezes and then starts again. We have become one of the shoppers, discussing the events, sharing a parent's concern. '

Having looked at the student's response, which shows you how to move a Level 3 response up to a Level 4, complete the following activity.

Activity 9

a Look again at your own response to Activity 7. With a partner, decide which level it fits into. Use the summary of the Mark Scheme opposite or the full Mark Scheme (page 37) to help you make your decision.

b Discuss which parts of your response you could develop in order to improve it.

c Rewrite your response, developing the parts you have discussed. Then re-assess your work with a partner to see if you would achieve a higher mark.

Level	Skill descriptors
Level 4	Shows **detailed** and **perceptive** understanding of *structural features*
Level 3	Shows **clear** understanding of *structural features*
Level 2	Shows **some** understanding of *structural features*
Level 1	Shows **simple** awareness of *structural features*

Progress check

So far, you have learned how to approach Question 3 by:

• identifying structural features

• selecting effective examples to support your answer

• commenting on them and analysing them using subject terminology.

a Now see how confident you are with these skills by completing the self-assessment below.

Skills	I am confident that I can do this.	I think I can do this but need a bit more practice.	This is one of my weaker areas, so I need more practice.
1. I can identify structural features in a text (and not confuse them with language features).			
2. I can select structural features to comment on and explain their effects on the reader.			
3. I can analyse structural features, using correct subject terminology.			

b Pick out one skill that you would like to target for improvement. Plan how you will improve that skill and monitor your progress. For example:

Plan – practise identifying structural features in a text, as opposed to language or content features.

Monitor – work with a partner at regular intervals to describe structural features of a text.

Try it yourself (on your own)

Re-read the Mark Scheme on page 37 (or the summary on page 46) before you start the following task to remind you what is being assessed.

Activity 10

Read the extract from *Transmission* below and write a response to the following Question 3 task, applying all the skills you have learned.

> You now need to think about the **whole** of the **source**.
>
> This is how one of the main characters, Arjun Mehta, is introduced.
>
> How has the writer structured the text to help you to learn about his character?
>
> You could write about:
>
> - what the writer focuses your attention on at the beginning
> - how and why the writer changes this focus as the extract develops
> - any other structural features that captured your interest.
>
> **[8 marks]**

In this extract from his novel *Transmission*, Hari Kunzru describes a young man, just out of college, attending his first job interview in New Delhi, India.

> Around him Connaught Place seethed with life. Office workers, foreign backpackers, messengers and lunching ladies all elbowed past the beggars, dodging traffic and running in and out of Palika Bazaar like contestants in a demented game. For a moment Arjun
> 5 Mehta, consumed by hesitation, was the only stationary figure in the crowd. He was visible from a distance, a skinny flagpole of a boy, hunching himself up to lose a few conspicuous inches before making his entrance. The face fluttering on top wore an expression of mild confusion, partly obscured by metal-framed glasses whose
> 10 lenses were blurred with fingerprints. Attempting to assert its authority over his top lip was a downy moustache. As he fiddled with his collar, it twitched nervously, a small mammal startled in a clearing.
>
> Finally, feeling himself as small as he would ever get, he clutched his
> 15 folder of diplomas to his chest, stated his business to the chowkidar[1], and was waved up the steps into the air-conditioned cool of the office lobby.

[Source text continues on page 48]

Marble under his feet. The traffic noise suddenly muffled.

Behind the front desk sat a receptionist. Above her a row of clocks,
20 relic of the optimistic 1960s, displayed the time in key world cities.
New Delhi seemed to be only two hours ahead of New York, and
one behind Tokyo. Automatically Arjun found himself calculating
the shrinkage in the world implied by this error, but, lacking even a
best estimate for certain of the variables, his thoughts trailed away.
25 For a moment or two the image hung around ominously in his brain
– the globe contracting like a deflating beach ball.

It was punctured by a cleaner pushing a mop over his toes.
He frowned at the man, who stared unapologetically back as
he continued his progress across the lobby. At the desk the
30 receptionist directed him to a bank of elevators. Stepping out at
the eighth floor, he walked up and down a corridor searching,
with rising panic, for Office Suite E. Just as he was beginning to
think he had been given an incorrect address, he came to a door
with a hand-written sign taped over the nameplate: INTERVIEWS
35 HERE. He knocked, received no reply, knocked again, then
shuffled about for a while wondering what to do. The shuffling did
not seem to help, so he kneeled down and polished his smudged
shoes with his handkerchief.

'Excuse me please?'

40 He looked up at a prim young woman in a peach-coloured salwar-
kameez[2].

'Yes?'

'Would you mind moving out of the way?'

'Sorry.'

45 She brushed past him and unceremoniously pulled the door open to reveal a waiting room filled with nervous young people, sitting on orange plastic chairs with the peculiar self-isolating stiffness interview candidates share with criminal defendants and people in STD-clinic reception areas. The woman swept in and announced herself to a
50 clerk, who checked her name on a list and assigned her a number. Consumed by his own inadequacy, Arjun followed.

The candidates squirmed. They coughed and played with their hands. They pretended to flick through magazines and made elaborate attempts to avoid eye contact with one another. All the
55 seats were occupied, so Arjun picked a spot near a window and stood there, shifting his weight from foot to foot and trying to reboot himself in positive mode. *Listen, Mehta. You don't know how many positions Databodies has open. Perhaps there are several. The Americans have a skills shortage. They want as many programmers as*
60 *they can get.* But such a number of applicants? There were at least fifty people in the room.

¹chowkidar – a watchman or gatekeeper (in South Asia)
²salwar-kameez – a traditional dress worn by women in India and Bangladesh

The language of evaluation

Here are some sentence stems that you can use when evaluating the text:

This makes the reader believe in the story because...

This makes us think of...

As we read this part, we feel... because...

We are shocked/surprised by...

This works because...

We recognize how the character must feel when...

The writer makes the character seem...

The impact of this sentence/description is...

Activity (2)

a Select one of the source texts listed on page 51 to evaluate. Use the notes that you made in the last activity and ask yourself the following questions:

  • How does the writer make me think or feel these things?

  • How well does he or she do it?

  Use some of the evaluation sentence stems in your answer.

b Compare your answer with someone who has chosen the same text.

Try it yourself (with support)

Now you are going to practise using your evaluation skills in a complete response to Question 4 on a text that you read on pages 47–49. You'll be given some support to help you do this.

Activity (3)

Re-read the extract from *Transmission* by Hari Kunzru on pages 47–49 and answer the question below.

Focus your answer on the second half of the source text (reproduced opposite).

A student, having read this section of the text said: 'The writer conveys exactly what it's like to go for an interview. You actually feel Arjun's nervousness, but it is the humour that I think makes it especially effective.'

To what extent do you agree?

In your response, you should:

● consider your own impression of Arjun's state of mind

● evaluate how the writer has used humour for effect

● support your opinions with quotations from the text.

INTERVIEWS
HERE

Behind the front desk sat a receptionist. Above her a row
of clocks, relic of the optimistic 1960s, displayed the time
in key world cities. New Delhi seemed to be only two hours
ahead of New York, and one behind Tokyo. Automatically
5   Arjun found himself calculating the shrinkage in the world
implied by this error, but, lacking even a best estimate for
certain of the variables, his thoughts trailed away. For a
moment or two the image hung around ominously in his brain
– the globe contracting like a deflating beach ball.

10 It was punctured by a cleaner pushing a mop over his toes. He frowned at the
man, who stared unapologetically back as he continued his progress across the
lobby. At the desk the receptionist directed him to a bank of elevators. Stepping
out at the eighth floor, he walked up and down a corridor searching, with rising
panic, for Office Suite E. Just as he was beginning to think he had been given
15 an incorrect address, he came to a door with a hand-written sign taped over
the nameplate: INTERVIEWS HERE. He knocked, received no reply, knocked
again, then shuffled about for a while wondering what to do. The shuffling did
not seem to help, so he kneeled down and polished his smudged shoes with
his handkerchief.

20 'Excuse me please?'

He looked up at a prim young woman in a peach-coloured salwar-kameez.

'Yes?'

'Would you mind moving out of the way?'

'Sorry.'

25 She brushed past him and unceremoniously pulled the door open to reveal a
waiting room filled with nervous young people, sitting on orange plastic chairs
with the peculiar self-isolating stiffness interview candidates share with criminal
defendants and people in STD-clinic reception areas. The woman swept in and
announced herself to a clerk, who checked her name on a list and assigned her
30 a number. Consumed by his own inadequacy, Arjun followed.

The candidates squirmed. They coughed and played with their hands. They
pretended to flick through magazines and made elaborate attempts to avoid
eye contact with one another. All the seats were occupied, so Arjun picked a
spot near a window and stood there, shifting his weight from foot to foot and
35 trying to reboot himself in positive mode. *Listen, Mehta. You don't know how many
positions Databodies has open. Perhaps there are several. The Americans have
a skills shortage. They want as many programmers as they can get.* But such a
number of applicants? There were at least fifty people in the room.

Having looked at the students' responses, and the annotations which show how to move up a level, complete the following activity.

Activity 4

a Look again at your own response. With a partner, decide which level it fits into. Use the summary of the Mark Scheme below or the full Mark Scheme (page 50) to help you make your decision.

b Discuss which parts of your response you could develop in order to improve it.

c Rewrite your response, developing the parts you have discussed. Then re-assess your work with a partner to see if you would achieve a higher mark.

Level	Skill descriptors
Level 4	Shows **detailed** and **perceptive** evaluation
Level 3	Shows **clear** and consistent evaluation
Level 2	Shows **some** evaluative comments
Level 1	Shows **simple** personal comment

Progress check

So far, you have learned how to approach Question 4 by:

- recognizing how the writer tries to achieve his or her effects
- deciding how effectively this has been achieved.

a Now see how confident you are with these skills by completing the self-assessment below.

Skills	I am confident that I can do this.	I think I can do this but need a bit more practice.	This is one of my weaker areas, so I need more practice.
1. I can understand what the writer is trying to achieve in the text.			
2. I can evaluate the effectiveness of the writer's choices.			
3. I can select relevant quotations and textual references to support my views.			

b Pick out one skill that you would like to target for improvement. Plan how you will improve that skill and monitor your progress. For example:

Plan — practise evaluating a writer's choices, by looking at a variety of texts, and using the language of evaluation

Monitor — work with a partner at regular intervals to read a text and practise using evaluative language orally.

Try it yourself (on your own)

Re-read the Mark Scheme on page 50 (or the summary on page 56) before you start the Question 4 task below to remind you what is being assessed.

Activity 5

Read the following passage from *The Other Side of the Bridge* by Mary Lawson. Write your own complete response to the sample question below, applying the skills you have learned.

> Focus this part of your answer on **line 12 to the end**.
>
> A student, having read this section of the text said: 'The way the writer describes the game really made me want to read on and find out more about the brothers' relationship.'
>
> To what extent do you agree?
>
> In your response, you should:
>
> - consider your own impression of the brothers and their relationship
> - evaluate how the writer describes the game
> - support your opinions with quotations from the text.
>
> **[20 marks]**

Arthur lives with his younger brother Jake on a farm. One day, Jake persuades him to play 'the knife game' in which players stand facing each other, about six feet apart, and take turns throwing a knife into the ground as close as possible to their opponent's bare foot.

> And so it was that on that warm July evening when he was thirteen or fourteen years old – at any rate plenty old enough to know better – Arthur found himself standing behind the line his little brother had drawn in the dust, waiting to have a knife thrown at his bare and
> 5 vulnerable feet. The dust felt hot, warmer than the air, and soft as talcum powder. It puffed up between his toes every time he took a step and turned them a pale and ghostly grey. Arthur's feet were broad and meaty with red raw patches from his heavy farm boots. Jake's feet were long and thin, delicate and blue-veined. Jake didn't wear farm
> 10 boots much. He was considered by their mother to be too young for farm labour, although Arthur hadn't been too young at the same age.

[Source text continues on page 58]

Jake had first throw, by virtue of it being his game and his knife. 'Stand at attention,' he said. His eyes were fixed on Arthur's left foot and he spoke in a hushed voice. He had a great feeling for the drama of the

15 moment, had Jake. 'Keep your feet together. Don't move them, no matter what.'

He took the knife by the blade and began swinging it loosely between finger and thumb. His forefinger rested easily in the blood runnel*. He seemed scarcely to be holding the knife at all. Arthur watched the

20 blade. In spite of himself, he felt his left foot curl inwards.

'Keep it still,' Jake said. 'I'm warning you.'

Arthur forced his foot to lie flat. The thought came into his mind – not drifting gently in but appearing suddenly, fully formed, like a cold hard round little pebble – that Jake hated him. The thought had never

25 occurred to him before but suddenly, there it was. Though he couldn't imagine a reason. Surely he was the one who should have done the hating.

The knife swung for a minute more, and then, in one swift graceful movement, Jake lifted his arm and threw, and the blade circled,

30 drawing swift shining arcs in the air, and then buried itself deeply in the ground a couple of inches from the outside edge of Arthur's foot. A beautiful throw.

Jake's eyes left the ground and he grinned at Arthur. 'That's one,' he said. 'Your turn. Move your foot out to the knife.'

35 Arthur moved his foot outwards to the edge of the knife and drew the blade from the ground. The skin on the top of his left foot was stinging, though nothing had touched it. He straightened up. Jake stood facing him, still grinning, arms at his sides, feet together. Eyes bright. Excited, but without fear. Without fear because – and Arthur saw this suddenly

40 too – Jake knew that Arthur would never risk throwing really close.

Arthur imagined his mother's face if he were to prove Jake wrong and slice off his toe. He imagined what his father would do to him if he were even to catch him playing this stupid game. He couldn't think how he'd allowed Jake to persuade him. He must have been mad.

45 'Come on,' Jake said. 'Come on come on come on! Close as you can!'

Arthur held the knife by the blade, as Jake had done, but it was hard to relax his fingers enough to let it swing. He'd thrown a knife before and he wasn't too bad a shot – in fact a few years back he and his friend Carl Luntz from the next farm had painted a target on the wall of the

50 Luntzes' hay barn and held competitions, which Arthur usually won – but the outcome had never mattered. Now, the chance that he would hit that narrow blue-veined foot seemed overwhelmingly high. And then, all

at once, he saw the answer – so obvious that only someone as dim-witted as he must surely be wouldn't have seen it earlier. Throw wide.

55 Not so wide that Jake would guess that he was doing it deliberately, but wide enough to bring the game to a safe and rapid close. Make Jake do the splits in three or four steps. Jake would jeer but he was going to jeer anyway, and the game would be over, and Jake would have to leave him alone.

60 Arthur felt his muscles start to relax. The knife swung more easily. He took a deep breath and threw.

The knife circled clumsily once in the air and then landed on its side eighteen inches or so from Jake's foot.

Jake said, 'That's pathetic. Take it again. It's gotta stick in the ground
65 or it doesn't count.'

Arthur picked up the knife, swung again, and threw, more confident now, and this time the knife embedded itself in the ground ten inches from Jake's little toe.

Jake made a sound of disgust. He moved his foot out to the blade
70 and picked it up. He looked disappointed and pitying, which was fine by Arthur.

'OK,' Jake said. 'My turn.'

He took the knife by the blade and swung it back and forth, looking briefly at Arthur, and when their eyes met there was a slight pause
75 – just a fraction of a second – during which the knife hesitated in its lazy swing and then picked up its rhythm again. Thinking back on it afterwards, Arthur was never able to decide whether there was any significance in that pause – whether in that instant of eye contact Jake had seen into his mind and guessed what he intended to do.

80 At the time he didn't think anything, because there was no time to think. Jake lifted the knife with the same swift movement as before and threw it, but harder than before, and faster, so that it was only a shining blur as it spun through the air. Arthur found himself staring down at the knife embedded in his foot. There was a surreal split second before the blood
85 started to well up and then up it came, dark and thick as syrup.

*blood runnel – a groove in the blade of a knife to let the blood run away

Paper 1: Explorations in Creative Reading and Writing

Preparing for Paper 1 Section B Writing

What is the content and focus of this section?

The Writing section of Paper 1 is worth 40 marks (the same as for the Reading section).

In this section you will write your own creative text, demonstrating your narrative (story telling) or descriptive skills in response to a written prompt or picture.

The writing task will have a thematic link to the topic that you have read about in the Reading section of this paper. However, this writing task will require you to write in a different way or from a different angle from the source text in Section A. Do not be tempted to repeat what's in the reading source in your own writing.

How to use your time in the exam

In the exam, you will need to spend about an hour on the reading questions (Section A), which will leave you about 45 minutes for the writing task. You need to use your time carefully, dividing it up between planning, writing and proofreading your work. For example:

- 5–10 minutes to plan your writing
- 30–35 minutes to write your text in full
- 5 minutes to check your writing and make any final improvements.

What choice of writing task will there be?

In this paper, you will have a choice of two writing tasks and you need to respond to *one* of them. Do not attempt them both! For each exam there will be a choice of:

- two descriptive tasks

or

- two narrative tasks

or

- one descriptive and one narrative task.

Take care when writing your response, because descriptive and narrative writing are closely linked. If you are responding to the narrative task (telling part of a story), it may also contain some description. However, if you have chosen to respond to the descriptive task, the focus of your work will need to be clearly on description and *should not* include narrative features such as a series of events or dialogue.

> **Tip** ✓
>
> Remember that there will not necessarily be a choice of one descriptive task and one narrative task; you may have to choose between two descriptions or two narrative tasks, so you must be prepared for both.

Activity 2

a Choose one of the story openings you have written in Activity 1. Look at the second image provided from the film *Feral* opposite.

b Imagine some time has passed between the two images. Write a later fragment of your story.

Peer assessment

Activity 3

In small groups, compare your story openings and rank them according to power and effect. You may find it helpful to discuss the following aspects of your stories:

- What type of story opening is it (refer to the grid on page 70)?
- What is the overall tone and atmosphere created by the writing?
- Are the tone and style of writing consistent throughout?
- Are the ideas clearly stated?
- Is the writing imaginative and interesting, or rather predictable?
- Is the vocabulary varied and are different sentence structures used for effect?

Tip

In the exam, you will get marks for using a consistent tone, style and register in your writing. This means you need to establish the mood and 'feel' of your writing and maintain it throughout. Use this task to practise making sure that the later part of your writing matches the beginning.

In the exam you will be assessed on the content of your writing. (See page 62 to remind yourself of AO5.) Look at the summary of assessment levels for your content in the table below.

Level	Key words for assessment levels
4	Content – convincing, crafted
3	Content – clear, chosen for effect
2	Content – mostly successful and shows some control
1	Content – simple

This means using language features in a skilful way.

This means using vocabulary to create particular effects on the reader.

This means that some parts of the writing work well, but not all.

This means that the content needs to be more varied, interesting or ambitious.

6 Describing a character

Tip ✓

Note that this description is of a real person from a non-fiction text, but you can use the same writing skills to describe fictional characters.

One of the writing tasks in Paper 1 may ask you to describe a person or character, or you may wish to include a brief description of someone in your story.

There are many writing techniques you can use to make your description interesting and entertaining for the reader. Read the extract opposite from Alan Bennett's *The Lady in the Van*, where Miss S leaps off the page into the reader's head just as dramatically as she steps out of her caravan.

Verbs and adjectives combine to help us picture how the character moves.

Gives us a hint of where the character lives, which provides clues about her life

Miss S's daily emergence from the van was highly dramatic. Suddenly and without warning the rear door would be flung open to reveal the tattered draperies that masked the terrible interior. There was a pause, then through the veils would be hurled several bulging plastic sacks. Another pause, before slowly and with great caution one sturdy slippered leg came feeling for the floor before the other followed and one had the first sight of the day's wardrobe. Hats were always a feature: a black railwayman's hat with a long neb[1] worn slightly on the skew so that she looked like a drunken signalman or a French guardsman of the 1880s; there was her Charlie Brown pitcher's hat[2]; and in June 1977 an octagonal straw table-mat, tied on with a chiffon scarf and a bit of cardboard for the peak. She also went in for green eyeshades. Her skirts had a telescopic appearance, as they had often been lengthened many times over by the simple expedient of sewing a strip of extra cloth round the hem, though with no attempt at matching. One skirt was made by sewing several orange dusters together. When she fell foul of authority she put it down to her clothes. Once, late at night, the police rang me from Tunbridge Wells. They had picked her up on the station, thinking her dress was a nightie. She was indignant. 'Does it look like a nightie? You see lots of people wearing dresses like this. I don't think this style can have got to Tunbridge Wells yet.'

[1]neb – peak
[2]pitcher's hat – baseball cap

One part of the character's body is described in a detailed phrase

Series of individual items of clothing represent different aspects of the character

One or two other aspects of appearance are picked out for attention but there is no description of facial features or overall appearance – this is left for the reader to imagine

An anecdote about the character gives us a sense of her experiences and attitude

Activity 1

Using Bennett's description of Miss S as a model, write a response to the example exam task below.

> Write a description of someone you know or a character of your own creation. You should aim to introduce the character and his/her lifestyle and personality to the reader.
>
> (24 marks for content and organization, 16 marks for technical accuracy)
>
> **[40 marks]**

Tip ✓

Remember that even if you choose a real person to describe, you don't need to tell the absolute truth! The important thing is to make sure your language choices create a vivid, engaging picture of your character for the reader.

Student B

> Answer starts well, setting the scene and introducing a contrast.

> Good attempts to help the reader visualize the scene and create a celebratory atmosphere.

> There is some variation of sentence forms.

> Discourse markers add coherence and help to direct the reader's attention.

> Varied openings of sentences help to engage the reader.

The night before was quiet and still as usual. The moon shone, the stars glittered and the city cats owned the streets. What a contrast with the next night! People gathered in groups all over the city, drawn to the stadium like needles to a magnet. They were smiling and laughing and joyful, they didn't care that they had to wait to get in. The stadium rose up above them like a massive wedding cake. Lights shining from every layer.

The best seats were at the top. From there, they could see how light spilt over the central area, but best of all, you could see the thousands and thousands of others who had come.

A sea of faces were lit from underneath. The noise was incredible. Nearby I could hear excited chatter and actual words – "It will be starting soon". From further away came shouts and cries that couldn't be heard exactly, but the feeling was celebration and excitement. A few seats away someone started a mexican wave and we were caught up in the silliness of swooping up and down for a few minutes.

Then there was a fanfare of noise. Sound boomed around the stadium and the human noises died down, waiting for the next stage of the entertainment. Suddenly, lights exploded into the sky. The fireworks was beginning. Purples and green shooting up into the sky. The air was full of showers of colour and oohs and aahs of everyone watching. Red spots and blue sparks and golden lines everywhere in sight, it went on and on. There were showers of silver and yellow wheels turning round and round. At last, the final amazingly loud crack! The sky was completely lit up and everyone stared with mouth open.

But it was over.

Examiner's comments

AO5: The content is clear and matched to the task, with the focus on description successfully maintained through references to sights and sounds. Overall, a range of choices have been made for effect. Ideas are connected. Structurally, there is a development from the panoramic view of the whole stadium at the beginning, to specific descriptions of the fireworks later, and then the final one-sentence paragraph.

AO6: The writer seems a bit rushed at the end and some errors creep in (*fireworks was beginning*), but not enough to spoil the generally clear communication. Sentence punctuation is mostly secure and accurate. There is some repetition (*into the sky*) and confusion over pronouns (*they, you, I*) but spelling is generally accurate and there are some increasingly sophisticated language choices (*light spilt, showers of silver*).

This exam response is a Level 3 answer.

To improve and move towards Level 4, the student should:
- maintain a single consistent point of view for descriptive writing so that there is no confusion over who is doing the describing
- include an image or idea that weaves all the way through the text
- use a wider, more sophisticated range of vocabulary
- work towards a higher level of accuracy and using the full range of punctuation.

What are viewpoints and perspectives?

Before we look at any texts or questions in detail, we need to think about the title of this paper and the two aspects of reading that it examines:

● viewpoint

● perspective.

Viewpoints

The term 'viewpoint' refers to the way that a writer thinks or feels about a topic. This may be **explicit**, clearly stated by the writer, or **implicit**, implied by the tone and language used.

For example, a writer might visit Las Vegas and say:

'I hate Las Vegas. It is a terrible, tacky place and the casinos are only interested in encouraging visitors to lose all their money.'

Here, the viewpoint is stated explicitly. We are in no doubt about what the writer thinks.

Now read this short extract from Bill Bryson's description of his visit to Las Vegas:

> When you have been to one or two casinos and seen how the money just pours into them, like gravel off a dump truck, it is hard to believe that there could be enough spare cash in the world to feed still more of
> 5 them, yet more are being built all the time. The greed of mankind is practically insatiable, mine included.

Activity 1

a With a partner, discuss and note down the words and phrases that tell us what Bryson thinks of Las Vegas and how it makes him feel.

b When you have finished, compare your notes with another pair. What techniques does Bryson use to communicate his viewpoint to the reader?

Here are some of the words and phrases that you could have identified:

> This **simile** is very striking but it is ugly. We don't see a torrent of gold, we see 'gravel'. The word 'dump' implies something of no worth. It uses **bathos** to undercut the beautiful image of money pouring.

> The intensifier 'just' adds emphasis.

> The word 'pours' implies a torrent of money – almost like a natural phenomenon. We can envisage the money pouring like a river or stream.

> 'Spare cash' again sounds worthless and insulting.

> 'Feed' is **personification** and makes the casinos seem like monsters.

When you have been to one or two casinos and seen how the money just pours into them, like gravel off a dump truck, it is hard to believe that there could be enough spare cash in the world to feed still more of them, yet more are being built all the time. The greed of mankind is practically insatiable, mine included.

> By ending with 'mine included' we see that he feels that he is likely to be tricked into losing money too. He is no better than the rest of us.

> The 'greed of mankind' sounds Biblical. Bryson is judging us all, not just Las Vegas.

Read the conversation between two students below.

Student A

> He obviously hates Las Vegas.

> Yes, but kind of evil.

> He makes them sound ugly, though, as well as fascinating.

Student B

> I'm not so sure. I think he finds the casinos fascinating.

> ... but it's because we're all greedy. Otherwise they wouldn't make any money. We think we're going to win.

> Maybe he's sort of divided. On the one hand he thinks they're evil but on the other hand he's attracted to them.

Key terms

Simile: a comparison showing the similarity between two quite different things, stating that one is like the other for example, *His hand was like ice*

Bathos: an abrupt transition in style from the exalted to the commonplace, producing a humorous effect

Personification: giving something non-human, human qualities or emotions

Now let's look at what a 21st-century young woman has to say about the attitudes of the older generation. In March 2014, 16-year-old Jenni Herd read an article in *The Times* newspaper about teenage brains, which annoyed her so much she decided to write this letter.

Annoyed

Sir,

I am getting increasingly annoyed at the barrage of articles about teenagers, and the adults who keep trying to explain our behaviour ("Moods and meltdowns: what's inside the teenage brain?", Mar 1). 5

I am 16 and a straight-A student, like most of my friends. We are not as irrational and immature as adults seem to think. We've grown up with financial crises and accept that most of us will be unemployed. We no longer flinch at bloody images of war because 10 we've grown up seeing the chaos in the Middle East and elsewhere. Most of us are cynical and pessimistic because of the environment we've grown up in—which should be explanation enough for our apparent insolence and disrespect, without "experts" having to write articles about it. 15

Has no one ever seen that we are angry at the world we live in? Angry that we will have to clean up your mess, while you hold us in contempt, analysing our responses as though we were another species?

I would like adults to treat us not as strange creatures from 20 another world but as human beings with intelligent thought—a little different from yours, perhaps, but intelligent thought nonetheless.

Stop teaching adults how to behave around us, and instead teach them to respect us. 25

Jenni Herd

Activity 5

a What view do we get of young people and their concerns from Jenni's letter?

b Write a brief comparison of this letter with *The Girl of the Period* on page 103. Are there any aspects that you think the young people share? What makes them different?

c Discuss some broader questions raised by the two texts:

- Could Jenni have written a similar letter in 1880 and would it have been published?

- Could any of Eliza Lynn Linton's criticisms have been made of boys?

- Will the older generation always criticize young people? If so, why might that be?

- How might a young woman of 1880 have responded to Eliza Lynn Linton's criticisms?

- How do you think that our 21st-century perspective affects our reading of Eliza Lynn Linton's piece?

- Do you agree with Jenni's views?

d Which areas of modern life do you think might be regarded differently by the generations? For instance, how do your parents, grandparents (and perhaps great-grandparents) feel about smartphones? Discuss this question and any other examples you can think of.

Tip

The skill of comparison is explored in more detail on page 132.

Question 1

Key terms 🔑

Infer: reach an opinion from what someone implies rather than from an explicit statement

Interpret: explain the meaning of something in your own words, showing your understanding

What to expect in the exam

Question 1 refers to a section of Source A and is worth four marks. Like its Paper 1 equivalent, it assesses the first bullet point of AO1 and is designed to test that you can read a section of text and select pieces of information from it. Unlike Paper 1, however, this question is likely to use a structured format, such as a list of statements, some of which are true while others are false. You will receive a mark for each correct answer.

This is a relatively straightforward task, designed to help you get started; however, there are some possible pitfalls. Bear in mind the following:

- Some of the statements will refer to implicit information and ideas, so you may not be able to find an explicit reference to them in the text. You will have to **infer** and **interpret** (unlike in the first question of Paper 1, which will just ask you to identify explicit information).

- Make sure you read each statement carefully before you decide whether it is true or not. You may be nervous and more likely to misread, so don't rush.

- If you do make a mistake, questions like this can be hard to correct because you may be asked to shade in a square and 'unshading' it again isn't possible. Don't worry if you need to change your mind, though. Clearly cross through the box of the statement you wish to 'unselect'.

- The question will direct you to a specific part of the text, using line numbers. Make sure that you only look for information and ideas from the identified lines.

Selecting true statements

Let's look at how you can develop your reading skills for Question 1 in the exam.

First, you need to think about the kinds of false and true statements that the examiners are likely to write about a text.

Read the extract opposite from celebrity chef Nigel Slater's autobiography *Toast*.

My mother is scraping a piece of burned toast out of the kitchen window, a crease of annoyance across her forehead. This is not an occasional occurrence, a once-in-a-while hiccup in a busy mother's day. My mother burns the toast as surely as the sun rises each morning.

5　In fact, I doubt if she has ever made a round of toast in her life that failed to fill the kitchen with plumes of throat-catching smoke. I am nine now and have never seen butter without black bits in it.

It is impossible not to love someone who makes toast for you. People's failings, even major ones such as when they make you wear short

10　trousers to school, fall into insignificance as your teeth break through the rough, toasted crust and sink into the doughy cushion of white bread underneath. Once the warm, salty butter has hit your tongue, you are smitten. Putty in their hands.

Activity ①

a Here is one false statement based on the above text:

Slater hated his mother because she burnt the toast.

With a partner, write a further seven statements about this text. Four must be true and three must be false.

b Try out your statements on another group. Were they all clear enough to enable someone to decide whether they are true or false?

c Select the best eight from your combined list with the other group.

When you have completed this activity and decided on the statements that work best, think about the skills you need to use to decide if a statement is true or not:

● close reading of the statement

● close reading of the relevant portion of the text.

Implicit information

One false statement that you may have written could be:

Slater's mother doesn't care about burning toast

or its true equivalent

Slater's mother doesn't like burning the toast.

The fact that she is concerned about the burnt toast isn't stated in the text, but it is implied in the sentence:

❝ *My mother is scraping a piece of burned toast out of the kitchen* ❞
window, a crease of annoyance across her forehead.

We can *infer* that because she scrapes the toast, does it out of the window and has an annoyed expression, she has burnt the toast by accident and is cross about it.

Try it yourself (with support)

Now you are going to practise using the skills in a response to an example Question 1 task. You'll be given some support to help you do this.

Read the following extract from Laurie Lee's autobiography *Cider with Rosie*, and complete Activity 2.

When we arrived at last I was helped down from the carriage at the age of three; and there, with a sense of bewilderment and terror, my life in the country began.

5   The grass amongst which I stood was taller than I was. I had never been so close to grass before. It towered over me and all around me, each blade tattooed with tiger-skins of sunlight. It

10   was knife-edged, dark and a wicked green, thick as a forest and alive with grasshoppers that chirped and chattered and leapt through the air like monkeys.

I was lost and didn't know where to move. A tropical heat oozed up from the ground, 15 rank with the odours of roots and weeds. High overhead, birds screamed as though they were tearing the sky apart. For the first time in my life I was out of the sight of humans, alone in a world I could neither 20 predict nor fathom. I was lost and I did not expect ever to be found again. I put back my head and howled, and the sun hit me smartly in the face, like a bully.

From this daylight nightmare I was 25 awakened, as I had been many times before, by my sisters. They came scrambling and calling up the steep rough bank. Like shields between me and the sky, faces with grins and white 30 teeth each to be called up with a loud cry, they brushed off terror with their broad scoldings of affection. They leaned over me — one, two, three — their mouths smeared with redcurrants and their hands 35 dripping with juice.

'There, there, Laurie, it's all right, don't you wail any more. Come on home and we'll stuff you with currants.' And Marjorie, the eldest, lifted me into her long 40 brown hair and ran me jogging down the path, and set me down on the cottage doorstep, which was our home, though I couldn't believe it.

That was the day we came to the 45 countryside, in the summer of 1918. To me, and to the rest of the family too, all eight of us, it was the beginning of a new life. But on that first day we were all lost. I crawled across the kitchen floor through forests of 50 upturned chair-legs and crystal fields of glass. We were washed up in a new land and began to spread out searching for its treasures.

Activity 2

a Read the below discussion between Student A and Student B. They are discussing two statements about the extract. Which student do you think has the right answers and why?

   1) Laurie Lee's sisters were angry with him.

   2) Laurie Lee was often looked after by his sisters.

b Find *three* more true statements from the list below:

   1) Laurie Lee had previously lived in a city.

   2) No-one else in the family feels lost like Laurie Lee.

   3) At one point Laurie Lee thinks that he will never see his family again.

   4) Laurie Lee is frightened by monkeys.

   5) The family are like explorers in a strange land.

   6) Laurie Lee often played on his own.

Student A

> I think statement 1) is true, because the text says that they scolded him. That means that they told him off. They thought he was being a cry-baby.

> I don't know if Statement 2) is true or not. It doesn't say that this happened often.

Student B

> I disagree. They did scold him but it says 'scoldings of affection'. That's not really telling him off. They're 'like shields' he says – they look after him and make him feel better.

> No it doesn't say it explicitly but it says that they woke him 'from this daylight nightmare' and that this had happened 'many times before'. So I think they did look after him quite often. Statement 1) is false but 2) is true.

Activity 1

a What do we learn about a new inmate's experience of a Victorian prison from Source A on page 113? Notice that the writer focuses on three aspects of the experience:

- the physical details (what the prison and the accommodation was like)
- the relationships (with the guards)
- the process of induction (administration and learning the rules).

Use this chart to record your information under the three headings:

Physical details	Relationships	Processes
Dark and chilly	Warden is gruff	New inmates stripped and bathed

b When you have completed your chart, compare it with a partner's. Did you both select the same things?

Now read the extract below from the diary of a modern prisoner.

Source B

MONDAY 11 MARCH

Many people think that prison must be a terrifying place with lots of violent women locked behind bars. It isn't. My arrival at Holloway was smooth,
5 humane and expertly carried out, involving quick fingerprinting and the BOSS chair (Body Orifice Security Scanner), essentially a metal detector.

There was no strip search but there are rules. It was clear I had brought in far too many clothes. I
10 was allowed to keep just 12 tops (shirts, T-shirts and jumpers) and six bottoms (trousers, tracksuit bottoms and pyjamas).

No toiletries were allowed but I was given an emergency bag with prison issue and I bought
15 a 'welcome' bag for £2.99, which would be subtracted from the cash I brought in with me.

It contained a bottle of orange squash, biscuits, a bar of milk chocolate, deodorant, toothbrush and toothpaste, a comb and some tea bags and sugar. I
20 had the choice of that or a smoker's bag. But I could take in my books, all 18 of them and many given to me by my children, as well as my writing pads and a couple of pens.

The welcome group and prison guards helped me and some other new inmates move our personal   25
belongings, which had been transferred into transparent prison plastic bags, to landing A3, the reception landing, which ended up being my home for the next few days.

The lovely girl who had secured the food for me told   30
me on the way that she had two more years to do but enjoyed doing the reception work because it kept her out of her cell until quite late in the evening.

That night was bitterly cold and I soon realised that the windows in Holloway cells do little to keep the   35
chill out.

At first I was shown a cell with no curtains and my helpers tried to fasten an orange blanket on to the railings, without much success. Fortunately there was another single cell available with curtains, this   40
time near the guards' office, but the TV was not working so there was another quick changeover.

Then it was obvious that one thin orange blanket on the bed was not enough. Soon the girls were at my cell door with extra blankets even though that was   45
apparently not normally allowed; within a few

minutes I ended up with five and had to turn down the offer of a sixth.

And then extra fruit and sandwiches that the girls must have had in their own cells started arriving, and shampoo for the shower and extra toilet roll for the loo in my cell. I couldn't believe the kindness of them all.

Many have commented about the solidarity in women's prisons – yes, there is bitching and some bullying but there is also a lot more demonstrable empathy among the women prisoners than in a men's prison.

They say that when that first lock-up happens and you are left alone in your room, reality finally takes its toll; when they finally lie in bed most new prisoners turn their heads towards the wall and start crying.

I watched the coverage of my case on TV and fell promptly asleep.

THURSDAY 14 MARCH

In the morning, a female guard from a different floor told me that there had been discussion for me to move to D0, the enhanced wing on the ground floor.

I told her I was happy to stay where I was for the time being. Frankly, I had already become friendly with the girls on my landing and had no wish to move.

And I had learned quite a lot of things from them – for example, how to put a pin on the latch door and pull it shut, or almost shut, from the inside if someone had left the hatch open and the lights on in the corridor through the night. This also cut out noise. Strangely, it gave you a feeling of being in control, which was welcome.

At the same time the girls showed me what to do if an overzealous guard had locked the latch door and there was no one there to unlock it – the back of the plastic spoon worked very well as a key.

A morning spent outside my cell, given the horror stories of very long lock-ups endured by many prisoners, was a relief.

I went to see the lovely nurse, and an instant friendship developed. She filled in my personal medical history details, checked my blood pressure (which had gone down sharply after a couple of nights in Holloway) and suggested I should have a hepatitis B injection.

I at first refused as I don't much like needles but she explained it was for my protection in case an inmate were to bite me.

There are a lot of drug addicts in prison who may be carrying the virus from infected needles. After her explanation, I did not hesitate for an instant.

My children came that Thursday afternoon for an hour. It was a tightly supervised setting, but it was brilliant. We had to sit opposite each other after we kissed and I reassured them that I was OK.

There were strict rules about moving around so we had to stay in our seats except when they got me a much-needed cup of coffee. I wasn't allowed to do it myself.

It was the first I'd had since I went into Holloway, so quite a treat for a coffee addict.

Activity 2

a Using the same table, repeat Activity 1 for Source B on pages 114–115 to collate information about modern prisons. (You may find it helpful to record details about the modern prison in a different colour.) As you work through this task, you will see that the experience of a modern prison is very different from a Victorian one.

b Now that you have all your information gathered together, you need to synthesize it – to bring it together, looking for differences between the Victorian prison and the modern one.

Using your notes from the 'Processes' column, write a paragraph showing the differences between the two experiences. You'll need to use some linking words, phrases and sentences to join them together, such as: *whereas, unlike, but, however, on the other hand*.

For example, your notes in the 'Processes' column might look like this:

> Arrival at a modern prison contains no strip search, just fingerprinting and a metal detector.
>
> The Victorian prisoner was stripped naked, all his clothes were searched and he had to take a bath in front of the warden.

By adding a connecting sentence, you could create this paragraph:

> Arrival at a modern prison contains no strip search, just fingerprinting and a metal detector. **The poor Victorian prisoner, however, was treated very differently.** He was stripped naked, all his clothes were searched and he had to take a bath in front of the warden.

Notice how the sentence *'The poor Victorian prisoner, however, was treated very differently'* enables you to link (synthesize) the two groups of information.

c In order to achieve marks for Question 2 in the exam you need some quotations to support the points that you are making. Select one quotation from each text and write out your paragraph to include them.

d Compare your choice of quotations with others in the class and discuss which ones are most effective.

Activity ③

a Now look back at your chart from Activity 2. Choose some information from either the 'Physical details' or 'Relationships' boxes to complete a synthesized paragraph including information about both prisons, supported by quotations.

b Swap your paragraph with another student and decide whether they have achieved the following:

- gathered information from both texts
- used linking language to show differences
- included quotations from both texts to support the points made.

Read the example exam question below, then look carefully at the extracts from two student responses below and on page 118.

> You need to refer to **Source A** and **Source B** for this question:
>
> Use details from both sources. Write a summary of the differences between the Victorian staff and the modern staff in their attitude towards prisoners.

Student A

Attempts to link evidence between texts.

Attempts some inference.

Identifies some differences.

The modern prison guards seem quite friendly, 'humane' and 'helpful' whereas the Victorian warden is 'gruff' and threatening, 'If I find you on it again I'll have you up before the governor or stop your supper.' The Victorian warden and the modern guards treat the prisoners quite differently.

Selects some quotations and references from both texts.

Examiner's comments

This response would be marked as Level 2.

Tip ✓

Notice how both students' paragraphs use terms such as 'whereas' and 'on the other hand' to link their interpretations of the two texts. Make sure that you have a stock of these ready for the exam because there are two comparison questions (Q2 and Q4). There is a list of linking words and phrases on page 136. You may be able to add more. Be sure to discuss both texts equally. It's easy to write a great deal about one text and forget the other one.

Activity 4

Once you have read the extract from Vest's speech on page 127, complete the following example of a Question 3 task.

> How does the writer use language in his speech to influence the jury's view of the relationship between a dog and its owner?

Remember to comment on and explain the effectiveness of:

- words and phrases
- language features
- sentence forms

and to:

- support your points with relevant quotations
- use terms correctly.

Peer assessment

Activity 5

a Swap your response with a partner. Does your partner's response:

- select words and phrases as examples of language choices and explain their effectiveness?
- identify language features and explain how they contribute to the persuasiveness of the speech?
- comment on the ways in which some sentences have been constructed in order to manipulate the reader's response?
- include relevant quotations?
- use language terms correctly?

b Make some notes on what your partner has done successfully and what could be improved.

c Now spend a few minutes giving your partner some feedback on their work.

Improving your answer

Now read the following extract from a student response to the question in Activity 4. As it stands, it would be placed in Level 2 but the annotations show how you could improve the response by adding clear explanation of the writer's word choices, language devices and sentence forms. This would move it up to Level 3. You would not need to include all of these additions to move into Level 3; they are just examples of the sort of things you could say.

Add in: This adds suspense because the jury is waiting for him to refer to 'the dog'. Also add 'the repeated use of modal verbs reinforces the feeling that these dreadful things could happen to anyone'.

Add in: The metaphorical use of the word 'flies' suggests that a man can lose his money quickly, hurriedly – resulting in a swift change of fortune.

Vest begins his speech by not talking about dogs at all. Instead, he lists all the ways that a man can be betrayed. He makes each example sound as awful as possible – his 'best friend... in the world' becomes 'his enemy' and when he describes the children 'that he has reared with loving care' we see a picture of family happiness. But then it says they are 'ungrateful' so that makes it seem like the happiness has been destroyed. In the next sentence, he uses the words 'nearest and dearest' to describe friends and family and he builds up this picture of 'trust' and 'happiness'. Then the word 'traitors' is used which sounds very harsh and violent. The next two sentences about money are short and use commas to create rhythm. In the example about reputation he uses the word 'sacrificed' which makes loss of reputation seem like a kind of death.

Add in: The words 'friend' and 'enemy' in the same sentence are juxtaposed and in direct opposition to each other. This presents the idea to the jury, and the reader, that turning against the man is stark and irreversible. This makes the change seem horribly cruel.

Activity 6

Having looked at the student response above, which shows you how to move a Level 2 response to Level 3, complete the following tasks:

a Look again at your own response to Activity 4. With a partner, decide which level your response fits into at the moment. Use the Mark Scheme on page 124 to help you make your decision.

b Discuss which parts of your response you could develop in order to improve it.

c Rewrite your response, developing the parts you have discussed. Then re-assess your work with a partner to see if you would achieve a higher mark.

Activity 2

a Now, working with a partner, go back to Source A and write a paragraph comparing one aspect with Source B.

You should use the following words and phrases to link your points:

Linking words and phrases to indicate differences	Linking words and phrases to indicate similarities
Whereas	Similar to/similarly
Unlike	Like
But	As with the
However	Both
On the other hand	This compares to
This contrasts with/in contrast to	In common with

b Compare your paragraph with another group. Evaluate the paragraphs together and decide how effectively they begin to answer the question.

Activity 3

To help yourself to prepare for Questions 1, 2 and 4 in the exam, try this activity:

a Find a recent broadsheet newspaper and select an article from the features section.

b Read it quickly but carefully.

c Write a summary of the content in 60 words or fewer.

d Ask a partner to do the same and then compare your writing.

e Who has written the clearer, more detailed or more comprehensive summary?

You will find that if you do this regularly, you will get better at it.

Try it yourself (with support)

Now you are going to practise using all the skills in a complete response to Question 4. You'll be given some support to help you do this.

Look back over pages 132–135 to remind yourself how to approach the question, then read the source texts below and complete Activity 4.

Source A

Why we shouldn't wrap our children in cotton wool

My youngest daughter had a bad bike accident recently but it won't change my mind on the message I give my children

Tim Lott
5 The *Guardian*, Friday 25 April 2014

[…] Last week, I was cycling with my seven-year-old, Louise. She wasn't cycling – she was perched on the back of my bike, with her helmet on, holding on to my waist. We had travelled many times this way before without incident.

10 As I was cycling I heard a rasping scream. My daughter is a habitual screamer, but this was different. I braked immediately, but lost balance as she was shifting about so much on the back. The bike slowly toppled over. I was thrown one way, and Louise fell with the bike. She had been screaming because her ankle
15 had got mangled in the moving spokes of my back wheel.

I lifted her and put her on my lap and inspected her wound. It was horrible. Huge and grey and blue and red and traumatised. The wheel spokes had ripped her shoe and sock off, leaving her bare flesh vulnerable.

20 Fortunately, the accident happened outside the house of some friends in the area. They brought us in, as Louise wept pitifully and I held her in my arms, the awful vision of her lower leg tugging at the corner of my eye line. Then, in between her screams of pain, she looked at me for a moment, and said, with
25 absolute faith that I would be able to: "Help me, Daddy." And I couldn't.

Our friends drove us to my house, where my wife, who is a nurse, took her to hospital. Tests showed that there may have been a small fracture and her skin was flayed, and could turn necrotic[1]
30 if not watched carefully. All this pain, all these wounds, were down to me. Now she has to walk on a crutch until it improves – a matter of weeks.

Louise is out of hospital now and we are travelling to Mallorca, where she will not have such a nice time as she might, as she is
35 going to be confined to a pushchair and a crutch. When anyone asks her what happens to her foot, she answers: "I don't want to talk about it." I hope it's just the memory of the physical trauma and not her father standing helpless in the face of her pain.

I have always believed that fear of risk was not something to
40 inculcate[2] in children – to be over-precautionary and constantly reminding them that the world is a dangerous place. We never tell our children not to talk to strangers. We allow the 11-year-old to go to the shopping centre with friends, on their own. Sometimes we pile too many children than is strictly legal in the
45 back of a car. I am, in other words, a fairly lax parent, somewhat by choice. Perhaps that is just the rationalisation that I have always used to justify my behaviour.

And yet, and yet… Wrapping your children in cotton wool and living every day as if a multitude of dangers were each crowding out the other to get their fangs into them still seems to me an 50
unhealthy message to broadcast. If your parents allow you to climb trees, sometimes you will fall off them. If you're allowed to go wandering alone in a wood, sometimes you're going to get lost.

I feel awful about what happened. I certainly won't travel with 55
Louise on the back of my bike again. But I refuse to swing to the other extreme – to a world seen through distorting spectacles that show only hazard. No one goes through childhood without getting hurt. And I won't let the continuing pangs of my guilt prevent my children living a childhood where confidence, not 60
fear, is the wellspring of behaviour.

[1] necrotic – when cells or tissue in a part of the body die
[2] inculcate – teach (someone) an attitude, idea, or habit by persistent instruction

137

Try it yourself (on your own)

Finally, read the following source texts and write your own response to the sample Question 4 task in Activity 7, applying all the skills you have learned.

Re-read the Mark Scheme on page 132 before you complete the activity. The Mark Scheme will help you to remember what is being assessed.

it. But it was hard to kr
85   able to tell her or show
comforted by rememb
proposed for my moth
the house, and yet it al
this will ever come right

Source A

Cheryl Cole take note – my whirlwind marriage has lasted 27 years

The singer's wedding after a three-month courtship is not to be sniffed at.
Unlike my moth-eaten wedding dress, my marriage is still going strong

Julie Oakley | theguardian.com, Tuesday 15 July 2014

5   The news that Cheryl Cole has married her husband after a
three-month relationship came a couple of days after I came
across the dress I was wearing when I met my husband,
Robin, 27 years ago. I was 29, and I'd wangled the chance
of crewing on a yacht on the Round the Island Race. If we'd
10   had bucket lists in 1987, this would have been on mine.

However, on the ferry to the Isle of Wight a Tannoy called
me to the purser's office to receive a ship-to-ship message
that technical problems meant my sailing boat wasn't going
to arrive in Cowes or even be in the race. I was never going
15   to catch the last train back to London so I daringly decided
I'd try my chances at crewing on another yacht. Nervously, I
walked into the sailing club, where a very drunk young man
immediately approached me and introduced himself. Finding
out my situation he loudly proclaimed my sailing ability to
20   the nearest group of sailors and cajoled them into letting me
join their crew. Then, as I needed somewhere to stay for the
night, this quirky, embarrassing man helped me find a bed and
breakfast, kissed me goodnight, and that I thought was that.

But three months later, in Luton register office, I was wiping
25   smudged mascara from my eyes as I promised to spend the
rest of my life with him. In the intervening time I'd discovered
that Robin was kind, generous, physically affectionate,
completely without guile, and that I fancied him like mad.
Asking me to marry him, and as soon as possible, was the
30   most romantic experience I've had. Can anything be less
passionate than being engaged for years followed by spending
a year or more planning a wedding? I'd had a few relationships,
one or two quite serious, and so had Robin. My most recent
relationship, living with a boyfriend, had given me a bullet list
35   of what I didn't want from a man. Every problem, every flaw in
the relationship had been a reason not to commit.

My best friend and bridesmaid said to me the night before:
"Julie, you don't have to go through with this". It was
understandable. I was making a commitment to a man
40   who to most outsiders seemed to have absolutely nothing
in common with me. But I knew he'd ticked the few boxes
that were non-negotiable for me. Everything else would be
an exciting adventure. Marrying someone you've known
for a short period of time is exhilarating. The first few years
45   of the relationship, you're in love and in lust, and every day
you're finding out about each other. You don't even know
whether your husband likes eating peas. You've made a

lifetime commitment, so you simply find ways of dealing
with problems as they arise. And they did arise. That marital
promise to each other right from the start has meant that   50
we've regarded each problem as a challenge to overcome
rather than a reason to give up.

When I told my 22-year-old son I was writing this article
about why short courtships can lead to long marriages, he
said: "You've got to pretend to be blissfully happy." Blissfully   55
happy is a lot to ask for after a hilly ride of 27 years. But
creating a family together, and living and loving together, and
experiencing passion together is something worth having.
Despite its age, the dress in the attic is looking remarkably
good apart from a few holes where some animal has nibbled   60
it. I can't fit into it any more and it's very much of its era, so
it's going in the bin. However that's not a metaphor for our
marriage. If it was, I'd be repairing the holes, letting out the
seams, removing the shoulder pads and wearing it. And
Robin would be telling me I looked pretty good in it.   65

Activity 7

Complete the following Questio

Read the whole of **Source**

Compare how the two write
of being in love.

In your answer, you should:

- compare the different poi

- compare the methods use
  points of view

- support your ideas with qu

Source B

During the 1870s, Francis F
In this extract from his diar

Friday, 8 September

Perhaps this may be a

To-day I fell in love with

I danced the first quadr
5   innumerable mistakes,
quite wild through the fi
horse, but she was so g
suffering.

It was a very happy eve
10   what was in store for m
Thomas this afternoon.

Sunday, 10 September

I have been in a fever all
and miserable with unce

15   *Wednesday, 13 Septemb*

An ever memorable day i
Vicarage at 10 o'clock an
him on the lawn about m
Ways, means and prospe
20   Thomas on foot rather ne
the bridge over the Digedi
feelings I should cross the
The whole family at home
room to see me and I was
25   get Mr. Thomas away for a
said suddenly, 'Come out i
came into the room. I thou
looked conscious. Then we
garden, her father and I. I s
30   much surprised but I hope
I am going to say to you.'

'What is it?' he said eagerly
living* of Glasbury?'

'No, something much neare

35   'What is it?'

I was silent a minute. I was f
'I-am-attached-to-one-of-yo
Just as I made this avowal w

---

1 Approaching the writing task

> **Tip** ✓
>
> Do not just repeat ideas from the source texts in your own writing. The examiner wants to see your own personal thoughts, rather than those of other people. You will not get marks for repeating what is said in the source texts.

> **Key terms** 🔑
>
> **Perspective:** a way of thinking about something from a particular standpoint, e.g. at a particular time or place
>
> **Statement:** something expressed in spoken or written words. In the exam task, the statement may or may not be enclosed by inverted commas.
>
> **Point of view:** opinion, a way of thinking about something

Remember that the writing task will be linked in subject or theme to the two source texts in the Reading section. This means that you will already have spent some time considering other writers' viewpoints and **perspectives** on an aspect of this theme or subject.

In the writing task, however, you will have opportunity to express your *own* point of view. It may not be about exactly the same issue as the Reading texts, but it will be linked in some way. Your reading should have stimulated some ideas of your own about the subject or theme.

In the exam paper, you will be given an opening **statement**, (possibly in inverted commas, but not necessarily) in which someone is expressing their **point of view** on a subject. Then you will be given a writing task, in which you need to identify:

- the *purpose* of your writing (for example, to explain your own viewpoint)
- what *form* you need to write in (for example, an article, a letter, a blog, a speech)
- who the *audience* will be (for example, the general public, readers of the school website, parents).

Look at the sample writing task below. The annotations show how to identify key features of the task.

> This tells you the *form* in which to write. In your blog, you will be writing for a general audience and will need to use Standard English, with all the *text features* associated with it, such as correct grammar, punctuation and sentence formation.

> A statement which expresses a point of view. This is likely to be controversial, i.e. one that provokes a lot of different opinions.

> 'Some people make a lot of fuss about handwriting; surely it's what you write that matters, not how you write it.'
>
> Write an entry for your blog in which you explain your point of view on this statement.

> This tells you the *purpose* of your writing, i.e. to explain your point of view. Note that it asks for 'your' view, so it should be a personal response.

Activity 1

a Below is another sample writing task. Copy out the task and identify the statement, purpose, audience, form, and the relevant text features that you will need to use.

> 'It has been said that nowadays, young people spend far too much time watching screens and far too little time reading books.'
>
> Write a letter to a magazine of your choice in which you explain what you think about this statement.

b Compare your purpose, audience, form and the relevant text features with a partner to see if you agree.

Tip ✓

When approaching the writing task, some students find it useful to think of 'PAT' to remind them to think about purpose, audience and text features.

2 Planning your response

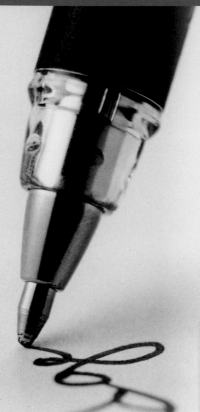

Before you start to write your response in the exam you need to plan it. This means deciding:

● *what* you are going to say (the content)

● *how* you are going to say it (the organization).

The content and organization of your writing is assessed in AO5, and is worth up to 24 marks (out of the total 40 marks for the writing task), so it is worth putting in some time and effort to plan carefully.

Your ideas for content

Plans can take many different forms, but most start with jotting down some ideas, linked to one or two main focuses.

Here are one student's ideas in a spider diagram, in response to the handwriting question on page 150:

'Some people make a lot of fuss about handwriting; surely it's what you write that matters, not how you write it.'

Write an article for a blog in which you explain your point of view on this statement.

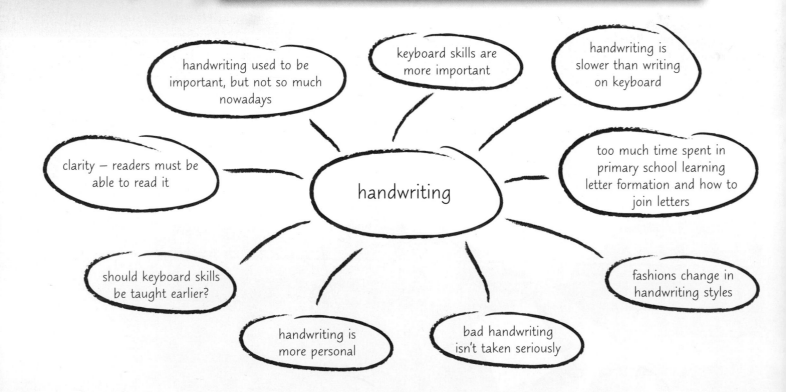

handwriting used to be important, but not so much nowadays

keyboard skills are more important

handwriting is slower than writing on keyboard

clarity — readers must be able to read it

handwriting

too much time spent in primary school learning letter formation and how to join letters

should keyboard skills be taught earlier?

handwriting is more personal

bad handwriting isn't taken seriously

fashions change in handwriting styles

Activity 1

a Now consider the exam question on page 151, and jot down some ideas for the content in a spider diagram.

> 'It has been said that nowadays, young people spend far too much time watching screens and far too little time reading books.'
>
> Write a letter to a magazine of your choice which you explain your point of view on this statement.

b Share your ideas with a partner, explaining your notes, briefly.

c On your spider diagram, add any key words or phrases associated with your ideas that you would like to use in your response. (These might come to mind as you talk through your ideas with a partner.)

Tip ✓

Remember that you will get marks for using a variety of interesting vocabulary, so jot down any significant words and phrases that occur to you during the planning stage.

Cohesive devices: techniques for connecting points, avoiding repetition and signposting arguments

Adverbial: a word or phrase that is used as an adverb and helps to link ideas together. A fronted adverbial is used at the start of a sentence and followed by a comma.

Discourse marker: word or phrase used as an organizational tool to link ideas

Pronoun: word used to replace a noun, often to avoid repetition

Reference chains: different words or phrases used for the same idea, person or thing many times in a piece of writing, like links in a chain

Structural features

As well as topic sentences, your writing should include linking words and phrases and structural features to add cohesion. Links *between* paragraphs help the reader understand the direction of each new paragraph compared to the last. Links *within* paragraphs show the reader how an argument is being built, say, through added detail, an example or an anecdote. Any parts of your writing that make links between and within paragraphs are known as **cohesive devices**.

The cohesive devices in the paragraph by the student who wrote about jobs and handwriting are shown here:

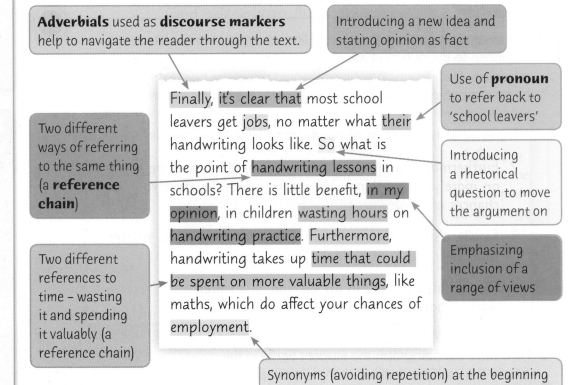

Adverbials used as **discourse markers** help to navigate the reader through the text.

Introducing a new idea and stating opinion as fact

Use of **pronoun** to refer back to 'school leavers'

Two different ways of referring to the same thing (a **reference chain**)

Introducing a rhetorical question to move the argument on

Two different references to time – wasting it and spending it valuably (a reference chain)

Emphasizing inclusion of a range of views

Finally, it's clear that most school leavers get jobs, no matter what their handwriting looks like. So what is the point of handwriting lessons in schools? There is little benefit, in my opinion, in children wasting hours on handwriting practice. Furthermore, handwriting takes up time that could be spent on more valuable things, like maths, which do affect your chances of employment.

Synonyms (avoiding repetition) at the beginning and end of the paragraph to reinforce argument

Activity 5

a Organize the discourse markers on page 163 into categories of your choice. Some of the words and phrases will be useful in more than one way, so might appear in more than one category. Some ideas for category headings are:

Category A – Good for starting new paragraphs

Category B – Good for going in a new direction

Category C – Good for building on a previous point

Category D – Good for pulling ideas together

b Add another linking word or phrase to each category you have suggested.

c Look back to your six-point plan for the answer to the exam-style question about young people and their screen habits (see page 155). Put some of your points into a sequence and practise using discourse markers to join them together. Example discourse markers are listed opposite.

Others may think that..., but what about...?   It strikes me that...   Some people argue that...

To summarize...   Finally...   As a consequence...   Provided that..., then...   Personally, I...

Whilst I agree that..., there is also a case for...   So, you see,...   It's clear to me that..

To begin with...   Secondly,...   Moreover...   It's important to remember that..., although...

Perhaps...   Let's examine this view a little more closely...   For instance...   It may be that...

In my experience...   It is certain that...   Some will disagree and say..., but I maintain that...

X (expert) agrees, stating that...   It's obvious that...   Should we really...?   Furthermore...

Everyone knows...

Activity 6

Read the following paragraph from a student response. It is clumsy and full of repetition. Rewrite the paragraph using discourse markers, pronouns and other cohesive devices to make it more fluent for the reader.

SPAG

> Watching screens doesn't do any harm. Watching screens can be a valuable way to pass time because people can learn things from screens like televisions. Young people use screens a lot because young people have phones, tablets and other gadgets with screens. But that doesn't mean that screens are damaging to young people.

4 Assessing skills for AO5

Now that you have looked at all the skills in detail, let's look at how they are marked. The grid below summarizes the Mark Scheme for AO5, showing the key words used for each level.

Level	Key words for content and organization
4	Content – convincing, crafted Organization – structured, developed, complex, varied
3	Content – clear, chosen for effect Organization – engaging, connected
2	Content – mostly successful and some control Organization – linked/relevant, paragraphed
1	Content – simple Organization – simple, limited

Now read the complete response from Student A, opposite. This is a response to the writing task in the exam-style question on handwriting, see below. Take note of the examiner's annotations and comments about this response.

'Some people make a lot of fuss about handwriting; surely it's what you write that matters, not how you write it.'

Write an entry for your blog in which you explain your point of view on this statement.

Remember that the examiner is only marking this response for AO5 skills – content and organization.

Student A

My handwriting is poor. It's an illegible scrawl that is not very different from when I was five. But should this affect my exam results, or determine the job I can get, or dictate my salary? Surely the content of my writing, and the quality of my ideas, is more important than the way letters and words are formed?

Some people would argue that a person's handwriting reveals their character. My mother, for example, is easily won over by beautiful penmanship. "Look at that handwriting!" she'll exclaim. "Whoever wrote that has a tidy mind!" Supposedly, handwriting features can be analysed to discover elements of personality, for example, by graphologists and criminal psychologists. However, this level of study of handwriting is a specialised skill being used in very particular circumstances. Most of us don't even notice the way a person slopes their letter ts or joins their cs to their hs.

In any case, keyboards are now omnipresent and typing skills are paramount. Perhaps this is the most persuasive reason that we should stop worrying about handwriting. Most people never have to write anything more than a shopping list these days, and even those informal notes to self and family can now be done through texts and reminder apps. Indeed, in the future, we won't even use keyboards for writing: voice-recognition technology is already included as standard on smart-phones and in some cars. Soon, all we will need for a day at school or work is a clear speaking voice and a gadget, and no-one will make a fuss about handwriting.

Even now, handwriting is much less important than it was. At primary school, I was made to practise joining my as to my bs over and over again, so that I could earn the right to use a pen. What a waste of time that could have spent on maths or other valuable subjects! Now, only a few years later, I complete all homework on a computer. Admittedly, in exams it is vital to have legible handwriting. But there are no extra marks for pretty writing and no marks are deducted for scribble. All that matters is that the examiner can read it.

I certainly think that while content is crucial, the way a person writes is irrelevant as long as it is readable. Beautiful, cursive writing may look pretty but all those loops and twirls can make it very difficult to read compared to a clear font on a screen or print-out. Nowadays, people focus on content; they don't make judgements about the appearance of your writing. Except, of course, my mother — so let's be grateful she isn't in charge!

Callout boxes:

- Pattern of three to emphasize points
- Rhetorical questions to engage the reader
- Ambitious and varied vocabulary
- Reference chains to avoid repetition
- General comments are developed and backed up by personal anecdote to increase engagement.
- Adverbials used as discourse markers to signal direction of argument
- Discourse markers to introduce and link paragraphs
- Link between beginning and ending

Examiner's comments

Overall the communication is convincing and assured. The tone and style consistently match the purpose, form and audience. This student has taken the topic seriously and included a range of points about handwriting. A more light-hearted tone has been introduced through the personal anecdotes, which helps to engage the reader. Structurally, the writing is well developed, with a variety of engaging complex ideas. A range of extensive vocabulary is used, with evidence of conscious crafting of linguistic devices. The student would be awarded a mark in the Level 4 range.

Now read the complete response from Student B, below.

Student B

Some discourse markers are used successfully.

Occasional attempt at more interesting vocabulary

Some ideas are linked and relevant.

Discourse markers are not always appropriate.

Rhetorical question

Firstly, handwriting something that only a few people care about and they are mainly teachers and parents. At work most people use computers to write reports and letters. This shows that caring about handwriting is old-fashioned.

Some people have to do good handwriting because other people have to read it. If a doctor writes instructions they has to be neat otherwise it would be unreadable. On the other hand, even though loads of time, is spent on handwriting lessons at school, not many people's handwriting matters.

At my primary school, the teachers were always moaning about terrible handwriting. But nowadays I hardly do joined up and none of my teachers seem to notice. Also, in the end, most people even with bad handwriting do get jobs. Although, this shows how unimportant handwriting is once you leave primary school. So what is the point of making people practise handwriting lessons in schools?

Handwriting is important but only sometimes, like when someone has to read it. But in most jobs being able to type quickly is a better skill. So prefrebly schools should teach people to use keyboards.

In conclusion, handwriting is not really relevant to todays society and I don't think we should make a fuss about it.

Examiner's comments

Main points are communicated with some success, using mainly simple vocabulary and some linguistic devices. There are some attempts to match purpose, form and audience; some attempts to control register. There are some linked and relevant ideas, and some attempts to write in paragraphs with discourse markers, although they are not always appropriate.

Activity 1

a Using what you know about the skills required by the Mark Scheme for content and organization, decide if and where Student B has shown the following skills:

- communication of ideas
- control over 'voice' (tone, style and register)
- ability to choose interesting vocabulary
- use of linguistic devices
- paragraphing.

b Looking at the Mark Scheme for AO5 on page 148, decide what level you think this student is working at.

c Discuss your thoughts with a partner. Together, prepare some feedback for Student B, suggesting areas for improvement, to increase their marks and achieve a higher level. Remember, your feedback should only focus on AO5 skills at this stage.

5 Practising key skills for AO6

This chapter will focus on the skills that you will be marked on for AO6.

AO6 assesses your ability to:

Use a range of vocabulary and sentence structures for clarity, purpose and effect, with accurate spelling and punctuation.

This means that you will be assessed on the 'technical accuracy' of your work. This is the nuts and bolts of your writing, how it all fits together and follows the accepted rules of grammar and spelling. However, following the rules isn't an end in itself – if followed properly, the rules mean that your writing is clear, accessible, precise and conveys to your reader exactly what you want it to. If your work is not accurate technically, it will be confusing, ambiguous and your writing will fail to really communicate or have any effect on your reader.

You can gain a maximum of 16 marks for the technical accuracy of your writing (compared to 24 for the content and organization). Although it accounts for less than half the overall marks, technical accuracy is nevertheless very important, so you need to think carefully about it as you respond to the written task.

In the Mark Scheme for AO6, technical accuracy is divided into six main areas:

- sentence demarcation
- punctuation
- sentence forms
- Standard English
- spelling
- vocabulary.

We will look in more detail at exactly what writing skills are involved in each of the above areas.

Sentence demarcation

Sentence demarcation is about how we mark the beginnings and endings of sentences. Every sentence must begin with a capital letter. For the end of your sentence you should choose the right punctuation, depending on the type of sentence.

- For a statement, use a full stop. For example, *Handwriting is a dying art***.**
- For a question, use a question mark. For example, *Is handwriting a dying art***?**
- For an exclamation or some imperatives (commands), use an exclamation mark. For example, *What rubbish***!** *Don't listen***!**

Activity 1

SPAG

Copy out and punctuate the paragraph below correctly, using capital letters, full stops, exclamation marks and question marks as appropriate.

putting a child in front of a screen — how lazy a screen is no substitute for a parent who can talk to a child, read to a child and play with a child on the other hand should we see screens as the enemy they can provide a good range of information and entertainment

To suggest that there is more to say at the end of a sentence, or if you want to leave the sentence unfinished, use an **ellipsis**. For example:

Perhaps handwriting is a dying art...

Key term

Ellipsis: a set of three dots showing that a sentence is unfinished. An ellipsis can also be used in the middle of a sentence to show that some words have been missed out.

Dashes

Dashes are used to separate clauses and introduce information or lists. In this way they do a similar job to colons and semi-colons, but are more appropriate in informal writing. It is acceptable to use them occasionally in exam responses, when you consciously want to introduce a less formal tone. For example:

Handwriting practice – an utter nightmare!

Beautiful handwriting might be something we aspire to – but not many have the discipline to practise.

Brackets

Brackets are used to enclose words or phrases that are afterthoughts, or that provide extra information. However, a sentence which uses brackets should still make sense if those brackets and the words contained within them, are removed. For example:

Handwriting practice (like other learning which depends on repetition) can be tedious.

Sentence forms

Using a range of sentence forms is essential to show you are in control of your writing. You should try to use a range of sentence forms for different effects.

Single-clause sentences (or simple sentences) are formed from one main clause. Longer, multi-clause sentences may be compound or complex sentences.

Compound sentences are created by joining two main clauses with a co-ordinating **conjunction** (for example, *for, and, or, but, so, yet, nor*). For example:

Handwriting is a controversial topic and it generates a range of views.

Complex sentences are created by joining two or more clauses with a subordinating conjunction (for example, *although, while, because*). A subordinating conjunction introduces a subordinate clause, which is one that doesn't make sense on its own. For example:

Handwriting practice does no harm, although some children might disagree.

Having the technical skills to express multiple points of view and counter-arguments will help you to get more marks for content (ideas) and organization (the way you organize these ideas). One balanced but powerful way to explain different views is in a multi-clause sentence structure, using conjunctions to link the clauses. This way, you can write one clause presenting one viewpoint, and another clause offering an alternative opinion. Consider these examples:

> **Key term**
>
> **Conjunction:** a word or phrase that joins words, phrases, sentences or ideas

Conjunctions link the clauses.

Main clauses, which could be written as simple sentences, express an alternative view.

While handwriting can still be important in workplaces, others would claim that the availability of technology means that touch-typing might be a more useful skill to learn.

Some may feel that a person's handwriting expresses their personality, although this could be disputed.

Commas are used to separate the clauses.

Subordinate clauses present one point of view – these are not main clauses because they would not make sense on their own.

Activity 3

SPAG

The following extract from a student response has been written entirely in single-clause sentences. Practise your range of sentence forms by rewriting it to include a variety of sentence forms. Add any additional words, punctuation and conjunctions that you need.

> Screens are versatile. They can be used for research, interaction and play. Books are less easy to share. Screen time has been linked to bad behaviour. Reading more books means young people are more successful at school.

Tip ✓

Short, single-clause sentences are very effective when used to introduce a topic or sum up a writer's feelings. They can make a particular impact after a long sentence.

| Tip | ✓ |

Occasionally, you may decide to use a well-chosen colloquialism in your exam, if it will help to reinforce a point or engage the reader. However, only do this to create a specific effect. The examiner will be looking for evidence that you can write fluently and consistently in Standard English.

Standard English

Paper 2 requires you to show your command of Standard English. This means following rules! Whether you are writing a blog, an article or a leaflet, Standard English will be required. Non-standard English generally describes how we speak, and should be avoided in exam answers.

Rules	Non-standard English (sometimes heard in informal speech)	Standard English (required in the exam)
Subject-verb agreement	*Teachers was always telling me to improve my handwriting.*	*<u>Teachers were</u> always telling me to improve my handwriting.*
Contractions	*Most younger people would say that handwriting <u>isn't</u> that important.*	*Most younger people would say that handwriting <u>is not</u> that important.*
Colloquialisms	*Handwriting is a valuable skill? <u>Yeah, right!</u>*	*Handwriting is a valuable skill? <u>Well, no actually, I do not agree.</u>*

Spelling

The mark for technical accuracy includes spelling. In this section, we will look at some common misspellings.

because, family, awkward, accidentally, argument, believe, height, immediate, mischievous, weird, until, realize

These words are often wrongly spelled by many students. You should record your own list of words that you have misspelled in your work recently, and then try to learn them. One way of doing this is to make up a sentence or mini-story containing all your key words (the sillier it is, the more memorable it should be) and practise spelling it until you are 100% right!

Here is an example sentence for the group of words above:

The family accidentally had an awkward argument because of their height. They believed they were weird until the mischievous elf arrived and immediately they realized they were normal.

Homophones

Homophones are words that sound the same but are spelled differently. This often causes confusion with spelling. Some of the most frequently misspelled homophones are listed below. Try to develop your own ways to remember them, but some tips are suggested below:

there as in 'over <u>here</u> or over <u>there</u>'
their as in '<u>the</u> <u>fir</u> trees shed <u>their</u> needles'
they're as in '<u>they are</u> going to spell <u>they're</u> correctly'

who's as in 'who is' or 'who has'
whose as in 'whose shoes are blue?'

you're as in 'you are'
your as in 'your birthday present'

Activity 4

SPAG

Review some of your recent writing, for English and your other subjects, and make a list of common errors in a notebook. Think of a personalized way to jog your memory for each one and jot it down. Ask a partner to test your spelling of the listed words at regular intervals.

Vocabulary

If you consciously upgrade your word choices in your writing, you are likely to upgrade your marks too. To be able to do this you need to expand your vocabulary through reading, listening and by looking up words that you don't know. Keep a notebook of new words and refer to it whenever you are practising your writing.

In the exam, you need to vary your vocabulary. A good technique to use in your planning time is to make a note of any word that you might need to use a lot in the answer. Then think of as many synonyms and related words as you can – these will help you avoid repetition. For example, for the question on handwriting, one student jotted down:

key word: handwriting

other words to use: joined-up writing, cursive writing, penmanship, calligraphy, writing style

Tip ✓

Don't let spelling be a barrier to your vocabulary choices. It's always better to choose a more ambitious word sometimes, and get it slightly wrong, than to stick to simple vocabulary for fear of errors.

Activity 5

Think about the key words you will need to repeat for an answer on young people's screen habits. You could choose 'screens' and 'young people'. Now make a list of synonyms and related words.

Examiner's comments

In Student A's response (page 177), sentence demarcation is consistently secure and accurate. A wide range of punctuation has been used with a high level of accuracy. The student has used a wide range of sentence forms for effect, and the level of Standard English is secure. Spelling is extremely accurate, despite the ambition in vocabulary choices. This student would be awarded a mark in the upper Level 4 range.

Now read the complete response from Student B, below.

Student B

Commas are used mostly successfully, for fronted adverbials and to separate clauses.

Firstly, handwriting something that only a few people care about and they are mainly teachers and parents. At work most people use computers to write reports and letters. This shows that caring about handwriting is old-fashioned.

Some colloquial phrasing

Some people have to do good handwriting because other people have to read it. If a doctor writes instructions they has to be neat otherwise it would be unreadable. On the other hand, even though loads of time is spent on handwriting lessons at school, not many people's handwriting matters.

Verb–subject agreement mostly secure but not always

At my primary school, the teachers was always moaning about terrible handwriting. But nowadays I hardly do joined up and none of my teachers seem to notice. Also, in the end, most people, even with bad handwriting do get jobs. Moreover, this shows how unimportant handwriting is once you leave primary school. So what is the point of making people practise handwriting lessons in schools?

Repetition of key words

Mainly simple vocabulary choices

Handwriting is important but only sometimes, like when someone has to read it. But in most jobs being able to type quickly is a better skill. So prefrebly schools should teach people to use keyboards.

Spelling error when more ambitious vocabulary attempted

In conclusion, handwriting is not really relevant to todays society and I don't think we should make a fuss about it.

A range of punctuation is used, although there are some errors.

Examiner's comments

Sentence demarcation in Student B's answer (page 178) is mostly secure and mostly accurate, and the student uses a range of punctuation, mostly with success. There is variety in sentence forms used for effect. The student mostly uses Standard English appropriately with generally controlled grammatical structures. The spelling, including complex and irregular words, is generally accurate and the student does attempt to use sophisticated vocabulary.

Activity 1

SPAG

a Using what you know about the skills required by the Mark Scheme, decide what level you think Student B is working at.

b Discuss your thoughts with a partner. Together, prepare some feedback for Student B, suggesting areas for improvement, to increase their marks and achieve a higher level. Remember, your feedback should only focus on AO6 skills at this stage.

7 Moving your writing up a level

Now you can use all the skills you have practised in this section by responding in full to an exam-style question. You can use any of the planning and drafting that you have already done in this section in your response.

Remember that you will be marked for content and organization (24 marks) and technical accuracy (16 marks). Use the table below to remind yourself of the key skills you need to show.

Content and organization	Technical accuracy
Communication of ideas	Marking the beginning and ends of sentences
Control over 'voice' (tone, style and register)	Using the full range of punctuation
Ability to choose interesting vocabulary	Varying sentence forms for effect
Use of linguistic devices	Controlled use of Standard English
Paragraphing	Accurate and ambitious spelling

Activity 1

Write a complete response to the sample exam question below, using the skills you have learned.

> It has been said that nowadays, young people spend far too much time watching screens and far too little time reading books.
>
> Write a letter to a magazine of your choice in which you explain what you think about this statement.

Activity 2

Once you have completed your answer to Activity 1, swap your work with a partner. Refer to the Mark Scheme summaries for assessment below, and feed back comments and suggestions for improvement to your partner.

Level	Key words for content and organization (AO5)
4	Content – convincing, crafted Organization – structured, developed, complex, varied
3	Content – clear, chosen for effect Organization – engaging, connected
2	Content – mostly successful and some control Organization – linked/relevant, paragraphed
1	Content – simple Organization – simple, limited

Level	Key words for technical accuracy (AO6)
4	Sentence demarcation – consistently secure and consistently accurate Punctuation – high level of accuracy Sentence forms – full range used for effect Standard English – consistent and controlled Spelling – high level of accuracy Vocabulary – extensive and ambitious
3	Sentence demarcation – mostly secure and mostly accurate Punctuation – a range used, mostly successfully Sentence forms – a variety used for effect Standard English – mostly used and controlled Spelling – generally accurate Vocabulary – increasingly sophisticated
2	Sentence demarcation – mostly secure and sometimes accurate Punctuation – some control of range Sentence forms – attempts a variety Standard English – some use Spelling – some accurate Vocabulary – varied
1	Sentence demarcation – occasional Punctuation – some evidence Sentence forms – simple range Standard English – occasional use Spelling – accurate basic spelling Vocabulary – simple

Sample Exam Paper 1

Source A:

In this extract from a short story, 'The Thing in the Forest' by A.S. Byatt, two little girls have been evacuated to the countryside during the Second World War.

The two little girls had not met before, and made friends on the train. They shared a square of chocolate, and took alternate bites at an apple. One gave the other the inside page of her *Beano*. Their names were Penny and Primrose. Penny was thin and dark and taller, possibly older, than Primrose, who was plump and blonde and curly. Primrose had bitten nails, and a velvet collar to her dressy green coat. Penny had a bloodless transparent paleness, a touch of blue in her fine   5
lips. Neither of them knew where they were going, nor how long the journey might take. They did not even know why they were going, since neither of their mothers had quite known how to explain the danger to them. How do you say to your child, I am sending you away, because enemy bombs may fall out of the sky, because the streets of the city may burn like forest fires of brick and timber, but I myself am staying here, in what I believe may be daily danger of burning, burying   10
alive, gas, and ultimately perhaps a grey army rolling in on tanks over the suburbs, or sailing its submarines up our river, all guns blazing? So the mothers (who did not resemble each other at all) behaved alike, and explained nothing, it was easier. Their daughters they knew were little girls, who would not be able to understand or imagine.

The girls discussed on the train whether it was a sort of holiday or a sort of punishment, or a bit of   15
both. Penny had read a book about Boy Scouts, but the children on the train did not appear to be Brownies or Wolf Cubs, only a mongrel battalion of the lost. Both little girls had the idea that these were all perhaps *not very good children*, possibly being sent away for that reason. They were pleased to be able to define each other as 'nice'. They would stick together, they agreed. Try to sit together, and things.   20

The train crawled sluggishly further and further away from the city and their homes. It was not a clean train – the upholstery of their carriage had the dank smell of unwashed trousers, and the gusts of hot steam rolling backwards past their windows were full of specks of flimsy ash, and sharp grit, and occasional fiery sparks that pricked face and fingers like hot needles if you opened the window. It was very noisy too, whenever it picked up a little speed. The engine gave great   25
bellowing sighs, and the invisible wheels underneath clicked rhythmically and monotonously, tap-tap-tap-CRASH, tap-tap-tap-CRASH. The window-panes were both grimy and misted up. The train stopped frequently, and when it stopped, they used their gloves to wipe rounds, through which they peered out at flooded fields, furrowed hillsides and tiny stations **whose names were carefully blacked out**[1], whose platforms were empty of life.   30

The children did not know that the namelessness was meant to baffle or delude an invading army. They felt   they did not think it out, but somewhere inside them the idea sprouted – that the erasure was because of them, because they were not meant to know where they were going or, like Hansel and Gretel, to find the way back. They did not speak to each other of this anxiety, but began the kind of conversation children have about things they really disliked, things that upset, or   35 disgusted, or frightened them. Semolina pudding with its grainy texture, mushy peas, fat on roast meat. Listening to the stairs and the window-sashes creaking in the dark or the wind. Having your head held roughly back over the basin to have your hair washed, with cold water running down inside your **liberty bodice**[2]. Gangs in playgrounds. They felt the pressure of all the other alien children in all the other carriages as a potential gang. They shared another square of chocolate, and   40 licked their fingers, and looked out at a great white goose flapping its wings beside an inky pond.

Glossary:

[1] **whose names were carefully blacked out** – during the Second World War, place names on stations and road signs were blacked out so that, if the enemy invaded, they would find it harder to know where they were

[2] **liberty bodice** – a kind of vest once worn by girls and women

Section A: Reading

Answer **all** questions in this section.

You are advised to spend about 45 minutes on this section.

0 1   Read again the first part of the source, lines 1 to 4.

List **four** things you learn about the girls.   **[4 marks]**

0 2 Look in detail at this extract from lines 4 to 14 of the source:

> Primrose had bitten nails, and a velvet collar to her dressy green coat. Penny had a bloodless transparent paleness, a touch of blue in her fine lips. Neither of them knew where they were going, nor how long the journey might take. They did not even know why they were going, since neither of their mothers had quite known how to explain the danger to them. How do you say to your child, I am sending you away, because enemy bombs may fall out of the sky, because the streets of the city may burn like forest fires of brick and timber, but I myself am staying here, in what I believe may be daily danger of burning, burying alive, gas, and ultimately perhaps a grey army rolling in on tanks over the suburbs, or sailing its submarines up our river, all guns blazing? So the mothers (who did not resemble each other at all) behaved alike, and explained nothing, it was easier. Their daughters they knew were little girls, who would not be able to understand or imagine.

How does the writer use language here to create a sense of danger and destruction in the coming war?

You could include the writer's choice of:

- words and phrases
- language features and techniques
- sentence forms.

[8 marks]

0 3 You now need to think about the **whole** of the **source**.

This text is from the opening of a short story.

How has the writer structured the text to interest you as a reader?

You could write about:

- what the writer focuses your attention on at the beginning
- how and why the writer changes focus as the extract develops
- any other structural features that interest you.

[8 marks]

0 4 Focus this part of your answer on the text from line 15 to the end.

A student, having read this section of the text said: "The writer really brings out the feelings of confusion and fear the girls had during their experience."

To what extent do you agree?

In your response, you should:

- write about the impression that you get of the girls' experience
- evaluate how the writer has created these impressions
- support your opinions with quotations from the text.

[20 marks]

Section B: Writing

You are advised to spend about 45 minutes on this section.

Write in full sentences.

You are reminded of the need to plan your answer.

You should leave enough time to check your work at the end.

0 5   Your class is compiling an anthology of writing about journeys which will be put on the school website.

Either:

Write a description suggested by this picture:

Or:

Write part of a story about a journey through a dangerous landscape.

(24 marks for content and organization
16 marks for technical accuracy)
[40 marks]

Sample Exam Paper 2

Source A:

Is there too much technology in our modern lives?

The Guardian, 10th April 2014

In our ever-increasingly electrified, automated world, Stuart Jeffries cries out for a more simplified existence

[…] As Britain powers down, you're sitting on the loo in the dark. You can't flush the toilet or wash your   5
hands because, when you upgraded your bathroom, you decided both should be electrically powered. As
you struggle with your trousers round your ankles to get outside and run your hands under the old-tech
water butt in the garden, you realise some unpalatable truths about the next few hours.

All 25 of your clocks will need resetting. You haven't got any briquettes to barbecue the meat that's
defrosting in your freezer […]. Your hard drive won't be recording Sue Perkins' **bon mots**[1] on *Great*   10
British Bake Off. All The Sims on your iPad are going to die because you can't care for them. Most
unacceptably of all, you realise, your phone battery's dead, you can't recharge it and so you won't be
able to tweet your outrage or update your Facebook status to angry (with an emoticon you're quite
fond of, featuring steam coming out of its ears).

And I will be there, tittering away. I want to front up. For years now I've been driven mad by the ever-   15
increasing electrification of our world. Without wishing to go the way of Bear Grylls […] in indicting
western decadence, the history of the decline of humanity could be written detailing the series of
putatively[2] labour-saving **prostheses**[3] that have saved us time, reduced distances and minimised the
need for human effort, but that have also ensnared us in lifestyles of idleness and fatuity.

When did it become too much of an effort for us to twist a tap on and off? Who invented the electric   20
tap and why haven't they been put in stocks for the public good? […]

Perhaps I'm going too far. But still. Every time I see a council worker with a leaf blower, I think
(fortunately using the silent inner voice that has spared me many a good kicking): "Sir, you have the
power in your hands to improve your life and reduce your waistline. Put down that battery-operated
instrument of Beelzebub and take up a rake."   25

True, he might well have an answer to that. He might well look at me as I walk down the street, head
down giving my attention not to the social niceties of pavement etiquette but to my email inbox and think
(using his own silent inner voice): "Sir, you have the power to improve your life. Put down that battery-
operated instrument of Beelzebub [he means my smartphone] and stop checking the football results/
texting your wife/emailing the optician/getting carpal tunnel syndrome from playing too much Tetris. Look   30
at the blossom, the children playing, the red sky promising a lovely tomorrow. Simplify, dude."

And we would both have a point. We have surrendered, not just our waistlines, but our dignity. So
much of modern life involves us standing absolutely still, like lobotomised privates on parade, while
technology goes to work. Don't move a muscle for the fingerprint reader! Don't blink before the retinal

scanner! Smile (fixedly) for the group selfie! Want to leave the shop with milk and muffins? Then   35
you'll have to hold the packages much stiller than that for the bar code reader, laughing boy. Have you
scanned your loyalty card? Taken the change? Told us how many bags you're using? Right: now take
your shopping and push off. Then we shuffle off, through automatic doors, abased and abashed.

Did we lose a war? Yes, we did but we didn't notice: the very things that we built to serve us, our
technological hand maidens, have made us servile. Truly, if cyborgs eliminated us now for the greater   40
good, we wouldn't have the right to complain.

Glossary:

1: **bon mots** – clever sayings or jokes
2: **putatively** – supposedly
3: **prostheses** – (literally) artificial body parts

Source B:

Fanny Kemble, a famous actress and singer was probably the first woman to travel by train.

A trip on Stephenson's Rocket, August 1830

… We were introduced to the little engine which was to drag us along the rails… This snorting
little animal, which I felt rather inclined to pat, was then harnessed to our carriage, and, Mr.
Stephenson having taken me on the bench of the engine with him, we started at about ten miles   5
an hour. The steam-horse being ill-adapted for going up and down hill, the road was kept at a
certain level, and appeared sometimes to sink below the surface of the earth, and sometimes to
rise above it. Almost at starting it was cut through the solid rock, which formed a wall on either
side of it, about sixty feet high. You can't imagine how strange it seemed to be journeying on thus,
without any visible cause of progress other than the magical machine, with its flying white breath   10
and rhythmical, unvarying pace… We were to go only fifteen miles, that distance being sufficient
to show the speed of the engine… After proceeding through this rocky defile, we presently found
ourselves raised upon embankments ten or twelve feet high; we then came to a moss, or swamp,
of considerable extent, on which no human foot could tread without sinking, and yet it bore the
road which bore us. This had been the great stumbling-block in the minds of the committee of the   15
House of Commons; but Mr. Stephenson has succeeded in overcoming it…

We had now come fifteen miles, and stopped where the road traversed a wide and deep valley.
Stephenson made me alight and led me down to the bottom of this ravine, over which, in order to
keep his road level, he has thrown a magnificent viaduct of nine arches, the middle one of which is
seventy feet high, through which we saw the whole of this beautiful little valley… We then rejoined   20
the rest of the party, and the engine having received its supply of water, the carriage was placed
behind it, for it cannot turn, and was set off at its utmost speed, thirty-five miles an hour, swifter
than a bird flies (for they tried the experiment with a snipe). You cannot conceive what that sensation
of cutting the air was; the motion is as smooth as possible, too. I could either have read or written.

Section A: Reading

Answer **all** questions in this section.

You are advised to spend about 45 minutes on this section.

0 1   Read again Source A from lines 1 to 19.

Choose four statements* below which are TRUE.

Choose a maximum of four statements.

A   There is no water because of a drought.

B   Stuart Jeffries believes we rely too much on electricity.

C   Stuart Jeffries thinks that Bear Grylls is right.

D   Stuart Jeffries will enjoy the power cut if it happens.

E   Stuart Jeffries believes that we have become controlled by technology.

F   Stuart Jeffries believes that we have used our technological skills wisely.

G   Stuart Jeffries believes that our lives have been improved by modern gadgets.

H   Stuart Jeffries believes that old technology is more reliable.   **[4 marks]**

0 2   You need to refer to **Source A** and **Source B** for this question:

Use details from **both** sources. Write a summary of the differences between the technology described in Source A and Source B.   **[8 marks]**

0 3   You now need to refer **only** to **Source B**, the description of the train journey by Fanny Kemble.

How does the writer use language to help you, the reader, feel part of her experience?   **[12 marks]**

0 4   For this question, you need to refer to the **whole of Source A** together with **Source B**.

Compare how the two writers convey their different attitudes to new technology.

In your answer, you should:

• compare their different attitudes
• compare the methods they use to convey their attitudes
• support your ideas with quotations from both texts.   **[16 marks]**

* Note, in the exam you will be asked to shade in a box alongside the statement.

Section B: Writing

You are advised to spend about 45 minutes on this section.

Write in full sentences.

You are reminded of the need to plan your answer.

You should leave enough time to check your work at the end.

0 5   'We have become slaves to technology and no longer engage with the real world around us.'

Write a blog for a website for young people in which you explain your views on this statement.

(24 marks for content and organization
16 marks for technical accuracy)
[40 marks]

Key terms glossary

Adjective: a word that describes a noun

Adverbial: a word or phrase that is used as an adverb and helps to link ideas together. A fronted adverbial is used at the start of a sentence and followed by a comma.

Bathos: an abrupt transition in style from the exalted to the commonplace, producing a humorous effect

Coherence and cohesion: the way that a piece of writing links together, in terms of vocabulary, phrases, clauses, sentences and paragraphs

Cohesive devices: techniques for connecting points, avoiding repetition and signposting arguments

Colloquialism: word or phrase used in everyday conversation rather than formal writing or speech

Colons: introduce a list. They can also introduce examples or explanations

Compound sentence: a multi-clause sentence which contains two or more co-ordinating clauses (clauses which could make sense on their own)

Conjunction: a word or phrase that joins words, phrases, sentences or ideas

Discourse marker: word or phrase used as an organizational tool to link ideas

Ellipsis: a set of three dots showing that a sentence in unfinished. An ellipsis can also be used in the middle of a sentence to show that some words have been missed out.

Explicit: stating something openly and exactly

Fronted adverbial: a phrase or clause that modifies a verb, which appears at the beginning of a sentence. It is often followed by a comma

Implicit: implied or suggested but not stated openly

Infer: reach an opinion from what someone implies rather than from an explicit statement

Interpret: explain the meaning of something in your own words, showing your understanding

Metaphor: a comparison showing the similarity between two quite different things, where one is described as the other, for example, The sky was a shimmering fabric full of sparkle and colour

Onomatopoeia: the use of words that imitate or suggest what they stand for, for example, cuckoo, plop

Paraphrased: reworded, explained in a different way

Pattern of three: the grouping of three words or phrases, used to create rhythm, or emphasis

Personification: giving something non-human, human qualities or emotions

Perspective: a way of thinking about something from a particular standpoint, for example, at a particular time or place

Point of view: opinion, a way of thinking about something

Preposition: a word used with a noun or pronoun to show place, position, time or means

Pronoun: word used to replace a noun (including proper noun), often to avoid repetition

Reference chains: different words or phrases used for the same idea, person or thing many times in a piece of writing, like links in a chain

Register: the kind of words (for example, formal, informal, literary) and the manner of writing that vary according to the situation and the relationship of the people involved

Rhetorical question: a question asked for dramatic effect and not intended to get an answer

Semi-colons: can separate items in a list, where the items consist of phrases rather than single words. They are also used to link two main clauses where they are both important or when you want to suggest a connection

Simile: a comparison showing the similarity between two quite different things, stating that one is like the other, for example, His hand was like ice

Statement: something expressed in spoken or written words. In the exam task, the statement may or may not be enclosed by inverted commas

Style: way of using language

Subordinate clause: a clause that gives more meaning to a main clause but does not make sense on its own

Summarize: to give the main points of something briefly

Synonym: words that mean the same thing or something very similar

Syntax: the order and arrangement of words and phrases to create sentences

Synthesize: produce something that has been blended together from different sources

Tone: manner of expression that shows the writer's attitude, for example, an apologetic or angry tone

Topic sentence: the sentence that introduces or summarizes the main idea on a paragraph

Verb: a word that identifies actions, thoughts, feelings or the state of being